Poems of the decade
An anthology of the Forward books of poetry
1992-2001

FORWARD
LONDON

First published in Great Britain by
Forward · 84-86 Regent Street · London W1B 5DD
in association with
Faber and Faber · 3 Queen Square · London WC1N 3AU

ISBN 0 571 20999 8 (paperback)

Compilation copyright © Forward 2001
Front cover illustration by Matthew Cooper

Reprographics by Vision · Milton Keynes

Printed by Bath Press Limited
Lower Bristol Road · Bath BA2 3BL · UK

A CIP catalogue reference for this book
is available at the British Library.

To Michael Meredith and Patrick Pietroni
but for whom…

Foreword

I CAME ACROSS the idea for *The Forward book of poetry* after being given
a copy of *The Guinness Book of Poetry* of 1959. It contained the best
entries to that year's Guinness Prize for Poetry. In it, delightfully, was
'Goodbye to the Mezzogiorno' by W H Auden and also poems by
George Barker, Charles Causley, Philip Larkin, Robert Lowell, Louis
Macneice, Sylvia Plath, Edith Sitwell and R S Thomas, as well as
contributions by relative newcomers to the poetry scene – Fergus Allen,
Thom Gunn, Ted Hughes, Jenny Joseph, Vernon Scannell and Iain
Crichton Smith.

What struck me about this collection was that many of the poems,
such as 'Goodbye to the Mezzogiorno', were to become classics that
would find their way into my life over the next 20 years of growing up.
Moreover, it presented a fascinating picture of life in the late Fifties,
painted in words by 70 or so poets. More than 40 years later, four of
those poets are still writing and are represented in this anthology.
Alongside them is the next generation of poets, some of whom will also
still be writing 40 years from now.

This anthology is about the Nineties. Ten years of poems drawn
from our recent past that tell their own tales about living in different
circumstances. Poems about Ireland, Iraq, Bosnia, Aids, sexual abuse and
homelessness, for instance, as well as the traditional themes of love,
dying, parents, childhood and nature.

I've selected the poems from ten years of entries to the Forward
Poetry Prizes. They span the last decade of the millennium and were
originally chosen by some 40 judges. Narrowing them down for this
anthology was an enjoyable but arbitrary challenge – in the end, I
decided to include just one poem by each poet and to feature each writer
alphabetically: A is for Abbs, Z is for Zephaniah, so to speak.

In terms of theme or date, this anthology has no structure, but I
suggest you read them as they appear – 127 poems by 127 poets from all
walks of life, written in the course of the last decade. Many of them are
already being absorbed by the generation currently in education.

This is an unashamedly personal selection. These are the poems that
have caught my attention, even though I may not have appreciated or
fully understood them first time round. Anthologies containing different

voices have that charm. Left by bedsides, in briefcases for journeys, or in lavatories, they can provide distraction from the intensity of our lives and be an expression of emotions that we feel, but may not have the language to express ourselves.

I would like to thank a great many people who have helped me along the way, especially the poets, editors, publishers and judges who have provided the contents of this book. A big thank you is also due to the various financial sponsors who, over the years, have contributed to the Forward Literature Trust that administers the Forward books of poetry, the Forward Poetry Prizes, National Poetry Day and Bedtime Reading Week. I'd also like to thank the organisations who have been our partners in these schemes: Waterstone's, Tolman Cunard, The Poetry Society, the Arts Councils of England, Scotland, Wales and Northern Ireland, and the BBC.

Lastly, I'd like to thank Ed Victor who got me started, Dotti Irving and her team at Colman Getty, and everyone at Forward who, through the years, have put poetry into everybody's lives with such enthusiasm.

William Sieghart

Publisher acknowledgements

Peter Abbs · THE MESSIAH · Winner, Western Mail International Poetry
    Competition 1991

Fergus Allen · THE FALL · *The Brown Parrots of Providencia* · Faber and Faber

Simon Armitage · The Two of Us · *The Dead Sea Poems* · Faber and Faber

George Barker · ON A BIRD DEAD IN THE ROAD · *Street Ballads* · Faber and Faber

Elizabeth Bartlett · ENTERING LANGUAGE · Winner, Staple Open Poetry
    Competition 1990

Connie Bensley · PERSONAL COLUMN · *Choosing To Be a Swan* · Bloodaxe Books

Michael Blackburn · ONE MORE · *The Prophecy of Christos* · Jackson's Arm

Eavan Boland · MOTHS · *In a Time of Violence* · Carcanet

Pat Boran · WAVING · *Familiar Things* · Dedalus

Colette Bryce · PHONE · *The Heel of Bernadette* · Picador

John Burnside · THE ASYLUM DANCE · *The Asylum Dance* · Jonathan Cape

Olivia Byard · THEFT · *From a Benediction* · Peterloo Poets

Matthew Caley · EIGHT WAYS OF LOOKING AT LAKES · *Thirst* ·
    Slow Dancer Poetry

Ciaran Carson · ALIBI · *Opera Et Cetera* · Gallery Books/Bloodaxe Books

Philip Casey · AND So IT CONTINUES · *The Year of the Knife* · Raven Arts Press

Kate Clanchy · WAR POETRY · *Samarkand* · Picador

Gillian Clarke · ANOREXIC · *The King of Britain's Daughter* · Carcanet

John Clifford · LUCK · PHRAS Competition Magazine, June 1993

Gladys Mary Coles · THE DORNIER · Winner, Aberystwyth Open Poetry
    Competition 1991 · Headland

Wendy Cope · Two CURES FOR LOVE · *Serious Concerns* · Faber and Faber

Robert Crawford · ZERO · *Spirit Machines* · Jonathan Cape

Iain Crichton Smith · THOSE · *Collected Poems* · Carcanet

Tim Cumming · BREATHLESS · *Apocalypso* · Stride Publications

Fred D'Aguiar · AT THE GRAVE OF THE UNKNOWN AFRICAN · *British Subjects* ·
    Bloodaxe Books

Sylvia Dann · BACK TO NATURE · *Back to Nature* · Jackson's Arm

Kwame Dawes · NEW NEIGHBOURS · *Progeny of Air* · Peepal Tree Press

Michael Donaghy · MY FLU · *Conjure* · Picador

Robert Minhinnick · TWENTY-FIVE LAMENTS FOR IRAQ · PN Review

Andrew Motion · FRESH WATER · *Salt Water* · Faber and Faber

Paul Muldoon · WIRE · *Hay* · Faber and Faber

Les Murray · The Shield-Scales of Heraldry · *Times Literary Supplement* · 1995

Stephanie Norgate · THE WHEEDLING MAN · *Fireclay* · Smith/Doorstop Books

Sean O'Brien · THE POLITICS OF · *Ghost Train* · Oxford University Press

Bernard O'Donoghue · HERMES · *Times Literary Supplement* · 1999

Sharon Olds · MRS KRIKORIAN · *The Wellspring* · Jonathan Cape

Alice Oswald · MY NEIGHBOUR, MRS KERSEY · *The Thing in the Gap-Stone Stile* ·
    Oxford University Press

Ruth Padel · CASCAVEL · PN Review

Don Paterson · NIL NIL · *Nil Nil* · Faber and Faber

Evangeline Paterson · LUCIFER AT THE FAIR · *Lucifer at the Fair* · © Estate of
    Evangeline Paterson

Brian Patten · THE ARMADA · *Armada* · Flamingo

Tom Paulin · DRUMCREE FOUR · *The Wind Dog* · Faber and Faber

M R Peacocke · GOOSE HYMN · *Selves* · Peterloo Poets

Pauline Plummer · UNCLES AND AUNTIES · Winner, Tees Valley Writer 1991

Peter Porter · TO MY GRANDAUGHTERS SWEEPING SPELSBURY CHURCH · *Collected
    Poems 2* · Oxford University Press

Sheenagh Pugh · ENVYING OWEN BEATTIE · New Welsh Review

Craig Raine · FROM A LA RECHERCHE DU TEMPS PERDU · *A La Recherche du Temps
    Perdu* · Picador

Peter Reading · AXIOMATIC · *Ob* · Bloodaxe Books

Deryn Rees-Jones · LOVESONG TO CAPTAIN JAMES T KIRK · *The Memory Tray* ·
    Seren 1994

Maurice Riordan · LAST CALL · *A Word From the Loki* · Faber and Faber

Robin Robertson · THE FLAYING OF MARSYAS · London Review of Books

Carol Rumens · BEST CHINA SKY · *Best China Sky* · Bloodaxe Books

Lawrence Sail · ANOTHER PARTING · *Building Into Air* · Bloodaxe Books

Ann Sansom · VOICE · *Romance* · Bloodaxe Books

Carole Satyamurti · STRIKING DISTANCE · *Selected Poems* · Bloodaxe Books

Vernon Scannell · VIEWS AND DISTANCES · *Views And Distances* ·
    Enitharmon Press

Jo Shapcott · VEGETABLE LOVE · *Her Book* · Faber and Faber

Penelope Shuttle · OUTGROWN · *The Observer* · 1995

Ken Smith · LOVESONG FOR KATE ADIE · *Shed: Poems 1980-2001* · Bloodaxe Books

Sam Smith · IMPORTANT INFORMATION FOR CANOEISTS · *Odyssey 16*

Stephen Smith · THE EXECUTION SHED · *The Fabulous Relatives* · Bloodaxe Books

Jean Sprackland · DEADNETTLE · *Tattoos for Mother's Day* · Spike · 1997

Gillian Stoneham · ELEPHANTS · Winner, PHRAS 94 Open Poetry Competition

Matthew Sweeney · INCIDENT IN EXETER STATION · *A Smell Of Fish* ·
        Jonathan Cape

George Szirtes · BACKWATERS: NORFOLK FIELDS · The Rialto

R S Thomas · GERIATRIC · *No Truce with the Furies* · Bloodaxe Books

Charles Thomson · RAMSGATE IN THE RAIN · *Something to Sling in Your Shopping
        Basket* · Yorick Books

John Powell Ward · SPELLING · *A Certain Marvellous Thing* · Seren Books

Andrew Waterhouse · LOOKING FOR THE COMET · *In* · The Rialto

Susan Wicks · MY FATHER IS SHRINKING · *The Clever Daughter* ·
        Faber and Faber

C K Williams · INSIGHT · *The Vigil* · Bloodaxe Books

Frances Williams · OYSTER EATING · *Wild Blue* · Seren

Hugo Williams · JOY · *Dock Leaves* · Faber and Faber

Edna Wyley · BOOKS, POETRY IN THE MAKING · *Eating Baby Jesus* ·
        Dedalus Press

Benjamin Zephaniah · MAN TO MAN · *City Psalms* · Bloodaxe Books

Every effort has been made to contact and acknowledge the source and/or
copyright holder of each poem. The Forward Literature Trust apologises for any
unintentional errors or omissions, which will be corrected in future editions.

Contents

Peter Abbs

THE MESSIAH

We had been waiting ever since we were born,
Crouched in the kitchen, where the ceiling flaked,
Or in the parlour with the curtains drawn –

As if home was the birth-place for a dread
That defied naming. The monologue of fear
Was in our eyes. Little was ever said.

Then as Spring was about to break each year,
A tall man arrived with a chalice of ash.
Thou art dust, he chanted in my ear,

And unto dust thou shalt return. With his thumb
He pressed the crumbling mark of Christ
Into our baffled flesh. My mind went numb.

We spent our lives with our knees on marble
In obscure corners with confessional voices
Heard just out of reach. Yet I was more than sure

We would be notified when the event came,
Receive an official letter giving a date
And a place, a number and a name.

Yet He arrived unannounced. A knock on the door
On another uneventful day and the Messiah
Stood there, smooth-shaved and assured.

He told us to leave things as they were.
We nodded. And assembled like Jews.
The kettle steamed into the air,

The dogs yelped and scratched at the door.
We lined up like cherubim.
It was the end we had been waiting for.

Fergus Allen

The Garden of Eden (described in the Bible)
Was Guinness's Brewery (mentioned by Joyce),
Where innocent Adam and Eve were created
And dwelt from necessity rather than choice;

For nothing existed but Guinness's Brewery,
Guinness's Brewery occupied all,
Guinness's Brewery everywhere, anywhere –
Woe that expulsion succeeded the Fall!

The ignorant pair were encouraged in drinking
Whatever they fancied whenever they could,
Except for the porter or stout which embodied
Delectable knowledge of Evil and Good.

In Guinness's Brewery, innocent, happy,
They tended the silos and coppers and vats,
They polished the engines and coopered the barrels
And even made pets of the Brewery rats.

One morning while Adam was brooding and brewing
It happened that Eve had gone off on her own,
When a serpent like ivy slid up to her softly
And murmured seductively, Are we alone?

O Eve, said the serpent, I beg you to sample
A bottle of Guinness's excellent stout,
Whose nutritive qualities no one can question
And stimulant properties no one can doubt;

It's tonic, enlivening, strengthening, heartening,
Loaded with vitamins, straight from the wood,
And further enriched with the not undesirable
Lucrative knowledge of Evil and Good.

So Eve was persuaded and Adam was tempted,
They fell and they drank and continued to drink
(Their singing and dancing and shouting and prancing
Prevented the serpent from sleeping a wink).

Alas, when the couple had finished a barrel
And swallowed the final informative drops,
They looked at each other and knew they were naked
And covered their intimate bodies with hops.

The anger and rage of the Lord were appalling,
He wrathfully cursed them for taking to drink
And hounded them out of the Brewery, followed
By beetles (magenta) and elephants (pink).

The crapulous couple emerged to discover
A universe full of diseases and crimes,
Where porter could only be purchased for money
In specified places at specified times.

And now in this world of confusion and error
Our only salvation and hope is to try
To threaten and bargain our way into Heaven
By drinking the heavenly Brewery dry.

Simon Armitage

The Two of Us
(after Laycock)

You sat sitting in your country seat
with maidens, servants waiting hand and foot.
You eating swan, crustaceans, starters, seconds, sweet.
You dressed for dinner, worsted, made to measure. Cut:
me darning socks, me lodging at the gate,
me stewing turnips, beet, one spud,
a badger bone. Turf squealing in the grate –
no coal, no wood.

No good. You in your splendour: leather,
rhinestone, ermine, snakeskin, satin, silk,
a felt hat finished with a dodo feather.
Someone's seen you swimming lengths in gold-top milk.
Me parched, me in a donkey jacket,
brewing tea from sawdust mashed in cuckoo spit,
me waiting for the peaks to melt, the rain to racket
on the metal roof, the sky to split,

and you on-stream, piped-up, plugged-in, you worth a mint
and tighter than a turtle's snatch.
Me making light of making do with peat and flint
for heat, a glow-worm for a reading lamp. No match.
The valleys where the game is, where the maize is –
yours. I've got this plot just six foot long
by three foot wide, for greens for now, for daisies
when I'm dead and gone.

You've got the lot, the full set:
chopper, Roller, horse-drawn carriage, microlight, skidoo,
a rosewood yacht, a private jet.
I'm all for saying that you're fucking loaded, you.
And me, I clomp about on foot from field to street;

these clogs I'm shod with, held together now with segs
and fashioned for my father's father's father's feet –
they're on their last legs.

Some in the village reckon we're alike, akin:
same neck, same chin. Up close that's what they've found,
some sameness in the skin,
or else they've tapped me on the back and you've turned round.
Same seed, they say, same shoot,
like I'm some cutting taken from the tree,
like I'm some twig related to the root.
But I can't see it, me.

So when it comes to nailing down the lid
if I were you I wouldn't go with nothing.
Pick some goods and chattels, bits and bobs like Tutankhamen
    did,
and have them planted in the coffin.
Opera glasses, fob-watch, fountain pen, a case of fishing flies,
a silver name-tag necklace full-stopped with a precious stone,
a pair of one pound coins to plug the eyes,
a credit card, a mobile phone,

some sentimental piece of earthenware,
a collar stud, a cufflink and a tiepin,
thirteen things to stand the wear and tear
of seasons underground, and I'll take what I'm standing up in.
That way, on the day they dig us out
they'll know that you were something really fucking fine
and I was nowt.
Keep that in mind,

because the worm won't know your make of bone from mine.

George Barker

On a Bird Dead in the Road

What formerly flounced and flew its fantastic feathers
Now lies like a flattened old leather glove in the road,
And the gigantic wheels of the articulated juggernaut lorries
Pound down on it all day long like the mad will of god.

Elizabeth Bartlett

Entering Language

Mothers remember the first word,
rising like a stone in a stream
of babbling. I hear the word *dot*
from my miniature pointillist
unsteady in his painted cot.
The first snow, and *Dots, dots, dots*
he cries with the eloquence and tone
of a lay preacher spreading the word
to a deaf world. We are as ecstatic
and amazed as Seurat discovering
the phenomena of vision. In his world
of wooden bars and hemispheres
of milky white, dots surround us
for a few days, stars are pin-heads
at night, sugar glacial specks;
we dot and carry one, hear Morse code
in our sleep, wake on the dot of six.
There's no doubt we are all dotty,
but soon we are into language,
no pause each day for breath;
linked words, sentences gather momentum.
Dots all gone away, he greets the sun.
We welcome him into our world; he picks
out commas, colons and full-stops
to please us, but Os are more exciting.
Oh, we cry to everything, but it palls
at last; the Great Os of Advent
turn into yawns. At dawn we hear him
trying out the seven antiphons and groan.

Connie Bensley

PERSONAL COLUMN

Married man would like to meet
girl, affectionate, petite,
for afternoon diversion.

Vicar sighs. He'd like to meet
married man. It's wrong to cheat:
he hopes for a conversion.

Jane writes off from school to meet
married man. He sounds so sweet
she longs for the excursion.

Blackmailer would like to meet
married man, to make discreet
enquiries re perversion.

Now his wife would like to meet
man – her eyes are cold as sleet –
she writes: I am a blonde, petite,
and spoiling for diversion.

Michael Blackburn

One More

one more rush of wind on a crowded platform,
one more drunk asleep on a bench,
one more nutter with a blitzed brain screaming,
one more smashed-up telephone, one more night of sirens,
one more ruck of skins shouting *kill the niggers*,
one more stranger's malevolent stare,
one more room at a criminal rent, one more landlord
trying it on, one more late train not arriving,
one more barman passing short change, one more
middle-class pig pushing in with his girlfriend,
one more pimp giving a Soho wink, one more pervert
buying in flashcubes, one more corpse for the river police,
one more trip to the social, one more time

Eavan Boland

MOTHS

Tonight the air smells of cut grass.
Apples rust on the branches. Already summer is
a place mislaid between expectation and memory.

This has been a summer of moths.
Their moment of truth comes well after dark.
Then they reveal themselves at our window-
ledges and sills as a pinpoint. A glimmer.

The books I look up about them are full of legends:
ghost-swift moths with their dancing assemblies at dusk.
Their courtship swarms. How some kinds may steer by the moon.

The moon is up. The back windows are wide open.
Mid-July light fills the neighbourhood. I stand by the hedge.

Once again they are near the windowsill –
fluttering past the fuchsia and the lavender,
which is knee-high, and too blue to warn them

they will fall down without knowing how
or why what they steered by became, suddenly,
what they crackled and burned around. They will perish –

I am perishing – on the edge and at the threshold of
the moment all nature fears and tends towards:

the stealing of the light. Ingenious facsimile.

And the kitchen bulb which beckons them makes
my child's shadow longer than my own.

Pat Boran

WAVING

As a child I waved to people I didn't know.
I waved from passing cars, school buses,
second-floor windows, or from the street
to secretaries trapped in offices above.
When policemen motioned my father on
past the scene of the crime or an army checkpoint,
I waved back from the back seat. I loved to wave.
I saw the world disappear into a funnel
of perspective, like the reflection in a bath
sucked into a single point when the water
drains. I waved in greeting at things that vanished
into points. I waved to say, 'I see you: can you see me?'

I loved 'the notion of an ocean' that could wave,
of a sea that rose up to see the onlooker
standing on the beach. And though the sea
came towards the beach, it was a different sea
when it arrived; the onlooker too had changed.
They disappeared, both of them, into points in time.
So that was why they waved to one another.
On the beach I waved until my arms hurt.

My mother waved her hair sometimes. This,
I know, seems to be something else. But,
when she came up the street, bright and radiant,
her white hair like a jewel-cap on her head,
it was a signal I could not fail to answer.
I waved and she approached me, smiling shyly.

Sometimes someone walking beside her
might wave back, wondering where they knew me from.
Hands itched in pockets, muscles twitched
when I waved. 'There's someone who sees me!'

But in general people took no risk with strangers.
And when they saw who I was – or wasn't –
they felt relief, saved from terrible disgrace.

Now it turns out that light itself's a wave
(as well as a point, or points), so though the waving's
done, it's really only just beginning. Whole humans –
arms, legs, backs, bellies – are waving away,
flickering on and off, in and out of time
and space, pushing through streets with heads down,
smiling up at office windows, lying in gutters
with their kneecaps broken and their hopes dashed,
driving, loving, hiding, growing old, and always
waving, waving as if to say: 'Can you see me?
I can see you – still... still... still...'

Colette Bryce

PHONE

Though we've come to hate this line
we call; stuck evenings when we've dried
the well of talk, we bide the time
in small long-distance silences
and lend ourselves as audience
to voices washed from tense to tense
across the middle air.

So, often, more than I can bear,
missing you brings this desire
at least to hear and to be heard
and then, there's something to be said
for this. For this becomes a web,
becomes a hair, a strength, a thread,
a harness between us, in all fairness,
you in my hereness, me in your thereness.

John Burnside

THE ASYLUM DANCE

At one time, I looked forward to the dance:
wandering back and forth in the quiet
heat of an August morning,
packing the car with cup cakes and lemonade,
boxes of plums or cherries, petits-fours,
nuts and spice cakes, mousse and vol-au-vents.
At noon I would go upstairs
to wash and change
– Sunday best, a clean white shirt and tie –
while mother made her face
and fixed her hair.
It was something we did, every year,
in that backwater town,
abandoning our lawns and flower beds,
to meet the patients, out at Summerswood.
It seemed a privilege to be allowed
within those gates, and know we might return,
to see the meadows, stripped with light and shade,
the silent lake, the fallen cedar trees.
We went there for the dance: a ritual
of touch and distance, webs of courtesy
and guesswork; shifts
from sunlight into shade;
and when the patients came downstairs
to join us, smiling, utterly polite,
in new-pressed clothes, like cousins twice-removed,
they had the look of people glimpsed in mirrors,
subtle as ghosts, yet real, with the vague
good-humour of the lost.
How we appeared to them, I can only imagine:
too solid, perhaps, too easy with ourselves,
sure of our movements, blessed with a measured desire.
All afternoon we picnicked on the lawn

then danced in awkward couples to the hiss
of gramophones, as daylight turned to dusk:
a subtle exchange in the half-light; acts of grace:
townsfolk conferring the weight of a normal world,
homes in the suburbs, the brisk lives of men who can who sleep,
the practised charm of women who believe,
who wake and forget what they dreamed, and go off to work,
and wish for nothing.
Beside the patients, we were lithe and calm:
we doled out charity and easy praise
and waited for the dancing to erase
the pain in the knot of the throat, the birdlike
angle of defeat against the spine.
We loved them for the way they witnessed us,
standing in twos and threes in the waning light,
made other by the rhythm of the dance,
the pull of a larger world, and that taste on the air
of birch-woods and streams: that knowledge of ourselves
as bodies clothed in brightness, moving apart
and coming together, cooling
slowly, as the lawns and rose-beds cooled,
heat seeping out from the skin and bleeding away,
the goldenrod turning to smoke
at the fence line.
Friendships began out there, to be resumed
year after year, the difficult months between
absolved by the summer light; and once,
a love affair, of sorts: an awkward boy
finding a girl, and leading her, mock-unwilling
into the lighted circle of the dance, to venture steps
that felt like steps on ice, the floorboards
creaking, and thin as paper.
They danced less than an hour, then she was gone,
and when he went back, next morning, the nurses
turned him away.
I think of her every day, I dream her skin,
and for years I have driven out, in the August heat,

alone now, with Mother gone, and my contributions
store-bought: jars of pickles; cling-wrapped bread.
I stand by myself, excused from the solid ring
of bodies and, for minutes at a time,
I see it all from somewhere far above,
some landing in the house, some upper room:
it makes me think of pictures I have seen
of dancers – wisps of movement on a lawn
at sunset: faces muffled, bodies twined;
the figures so close to the darkness, they might be
apparitions, venturing on form,
pinewoods above the lake, a suggestion of watchers,
a gap between night and day, between light and shade,
and faces melting, one into the next
as if they were all one flesh, in a single dream,
and nothing to make them true, but space, and time.

Olivia Byard

THEFT

Her childhood was thieved, not at night
when terrors beat wings, but while the sun
reared helpless against window panes
before falling hard from the sky's arms.
Since then she has mourned in a twilight
that lurks to catch dark.

The whole thing reminds her of rings
on men's fingers: tight rings that scratch flesh,
like chalk across a blackboard.
Even the memory of her own reflection
jars with its companion glass of
dentists' drills, blood in baths.

His legs were everywhere; his touch
a careless sting; she knows
she should no longer cringe, but,
helpless, screams at smallish spiders
that crawl on grubby porcelain. An old
thief stole her youth, junked it afterward.

Matthew Caley

1
From afar, like Ishtar, aloof
on some spectacular limestone outcrop,
through binoculars. You'll be suffering from a headache
beyond the reach of *Aspirin*. It is a headache-coloured sky
and the lake itself is a grey headache, an undistinguished lozenge,
part of a panoramic, cinemascopic sweep,
but boring beneath the sky's distemper,
small.

2
Imagine yourself a minor Lakeland poet,
far from his sister's tussock, plucking an albatross, nursing the itch
of syphilis. With his laudanum-phial and, of course,
his vellum-bound volume of verse. Things can only
get better after this.
Or worse.

3
Close-up. In sunshine. With everything holiday-brochure bright,
airbrushed even. Even. Catch the surface-spangles, gyres, spirals,
silvery ring-pulls, rivets, all chainmail-linked and glinting. Think
of the importance of surfaces. The planes of people's faces.
Be satisfied with shallows. Here clouds are mountains,
mountains clouds and sheeted lakes, inscrutable, mirror both.
For the adventurous, dip your toe halfway
up your toenail. For the gifted – get walking.

4*a*
Read W. H. Auden's *Lakes* [from *Bucolics*] and know all there is
   to know.
Almost. When you have finished, check the Ordinance Survey Map
of his face. Find solace in each fissure. Wallow.

4*b*

An ankle-deep paddle. We are 70% water ourselves. Little lopsided
waking lakes. Hardly amniotic. Hardly baptismal. Though
                    watch out
for suddenly sepulchral doves that come and go
in a tin-flash. And don't forget your socks
busy sunbathing on the bank

5

Skinny-dipping. Let the salt support you. Think how many salt tears
would constitute a lake. That cold gasp as lakewater hits your groin.
Dippings, siftings, bits floating off. Your umbilical now knotted
and not in service. Sun-spangles on your cellulite
and your runny, foreshortened legs, thalidomide in rivulets.
Drift off, a jungle-raft to Samarkand and

6

have sex like waterbabies spawning in the spray.
The more professional can water-ski or analyse the wave-raked silt
replete with collective guilt and plastic goggles. Find the greeny-blue
bodies of underage boys and girls barely recognisable
from the local Echo or Star. Lapping darkness. The moiré effect
                    of bubbles.
Deep, deep. You are diving too deep.

7

The one rule is 'everything ends'.
You now have a choice between the bottom or the bends.

8

This is the bottom. Grey-blue, billowing. Krakens, crud.
Long-missed Masons, rust. An underwater city of muffled bells
malingering beyond. Water or land. No-one can tell which is which.
When you finally set foot in Atlantis
its dust is dry to the touch.

Ciaran Carson

ALIBI

Remorselessly, in fields and forests, on street corners,
    on the eternal
Altar of the bed, murder is done. Was I there? I
    stared into the terminal

Of my own mirrored pupil, and saw my eye denying it,
    like one hand
Washing clean the other. Where was I then? Everybody
    wears the same Cain brand

Emblazoned on their foreheads. I saw the deed and what
    it led to. Heard the shriek
As well. And then my eyes were decommissioned by the knife.
    But I saw him last week,

And I know he is amongst us. And no, I can't tell his
    name. What name would you
Make up for murderers of their own childhood, who
    believe lies to be true?

The lovers enter the marrowbone of a madman and succumb
    slowly in their pit
Of lime. A croaking black unkindness of ravens has
    cloaked it

With a counterfeit of corpses. All our words were in vain.
    What flag are we supposed
To raise above the citadel? Where should we go? All
    the roads are closed.

O ubiquitous surveillant God, we are accomplices to
    all assassinations.
Gag me, choke me, strangle me, and tell me that there
    are no further destinations.

And finally, it must be left unsaid that those not born
    to this, our vampire family,
Sleep soundly in their beds: they have the final alibi.

Philip Casey

And So It Continues

Beyond the headstones in the graveyard
there is a special plot for limbs.
Severed legs and arms
mingle promiscuously in death,
if they missed their chance in life.
The hand of someone's husband
rests on the leg of someone's wife.

Kate Clanchy

War Poetry

The class has dropped its books. The janitor's
disturbed some wasps, broomed the nest
straight off the roof. It lies outside, exotic
as a fallen planet, a burst city of the poor;
its newsprint halls, its ashen, tiny rooms
all open to the air. The insects' buzz
is low-key as a smart machine. They group,
regroup, in stacks and coils, advance
and cross like pulsing points on radar screens.

And though the boys have shaven heads
and football strips, and would, they swear,
enlist at once, given half a chance,
march down Owen's darkening lanes
to join the lads and stuff the Boche –
they don't rush out to pike the nest,
or lap the yard with grapeshot faces.
They watch the wasps through glass,
silently, abashed, the way we all watch war.

Gillian Clarke

Anorexic

My father's sister,
the one who died
before there was a word for it,
was fussy with her food.
'Eat up,' they'd say to me,
ladling a bowl with warning.

What I remember's
how she'd send me to the dairy,
taught me to take cream,
the standing gold.
Where the jug dipped
I saw its blue-milk skin
before the surface healed.

Breath held, tongue between teeth,
I carried in the cream,
brimmed, level,
parallel, I knew,
with that other, hidden horizon
of the earth's deep
ungleaming water-table.

And she, more often than not half-dressed,
stockings, a slip, a Chinese kimono,
would warm the cream, pour it
with crumbled melting cheese
over a delicate white cauliflower,
or field mushrooms
steaming in porcelain,

then watch us eat, relishing,
smoking her umpteenth cigarette,
glamorous, perfumed, starved,
and going to die.

John Clifford

On the building site at midday,
We sat round a packing case
And played cards while the tea brewed,
Paddy and Tiny White and Neverfuck and me.
We laid down the cards, one by one,
Each card a day's life,
And tight in our hands we held the rest of our days.

Red days and black days were scattered on the box,
Put down softly or carelessly or with a bang;
And Paddy is crushed between a truck and a wall,
And Tiny White is unemployed and bitter,
And Neverfuck a sour wizened old husk,
And I have smooth hands and a soft job,
For so the cards were dealt and so they fell.

Perhaps with luck it could have been quite different;
Paddy happily drunk in a pub in Sligo,
Tiny in a suit, taking home real money,
Neverfuck happy in some peculiar way,
And for myself no need to feel a traitor.
That is how I would have dealt the cards
If I had known, and if it had been my deal.

But *these* are the cards, smeared with thumb marks,
Torn corners, hard used every day,
Like Paddy, Tiny, Neverfuck and me.
And this is the game, and this the building site,
And these the dirty times we live in;
And if we are going to change our luck and win –
This is where we must start.

Gladys Mary Coles

The Dornier

The moorland blazing and a bomber's moon
lit skies light as a June dawn,
the harvest stubble to a guilty flush.
I saw from the farmhouse the smoking plane
like a giant bat in a sideways dive,
fuel spewing from its underbelly.
I remember how one wing tipped our trees
tearing the screen of pines like lace,
flipping over, flimsy as my balsa models.
It shattered on the pasture, killing sheep,
ripping the fence where the shot fox hung.
Dad let me look next morning at the wreck –
it lay in two halves like a broken wasp,
nose nestled in the ground, blades
of the propellers bent...
I thought I saw them moving
in the wind.

If the Invader comes, the leaflet said,
*Do not give a German anything. Do not tell him
anything. Hide your food and bicycles.
Hide your maps.* ... But these Luftwaffe men
were dead. Their machine, a carcass
cordoned off. A museum dinosaur.
Don't go nearer. Do not touch.

Trophies, I took – a section of the tail
(our collie found it dangling in the hedge),
pieces of perspex like thin ice on the grass,
some swapped for shrapnel down at school
(how strangely it burned in a slow green flame).
Inscribed *September 1940, Nantglyn*,
the black-crossed relic now hangs on our wall.
My son lifts it down, asks questions
I can't answer.

Yesterday, turning the far meadow for new drains,
our blades hit three marrows, huge and hard,
stuffed with High Explosive – the Dornier's final gift.
Cordoned off, they're photographed, defused.
I take my son to see the empty crater,
the imprint of their shapes still in the soil –
shadows that turn up time.

Wendy Cope

TWO CURES FOR LOVE

1 Don't see him. Don't phone or write a letter.
2 The easy way: get to know him better.

Robert Crawford

ZERO

Thank you for calling Heatheryhaugh Nuclear Arsenal.
If your main lust is for weapons of mass destruction
Please try our other number in Inverbervie.

On your touchtone phone jab one for details
Of bombs that kill crofters but leave brochs and megaliths standing;
Two for snug dumpsites; three for pre-owned

Atomic oddments with warranties for several years;
Four for rucksacks of fissile material;
Five will patch you through to Glencora Gillanders,

Anthrax buyer for the Loch Ness and Great Glen area;
Six for the Arsenal's renowned in-house distillery;
Seven affords highlights of our unusual safety record,

Reassuring callers we are sited in a remote location,
Though, should you wish to visit, pressing eight provides
Pibrochs from this area of comical natural beauty.

Nine connects you to our twelve-hour emergency helpline
(Not staffed on Sundays, Hogmanay, or New Year's Day).
If this extension is busy, please yell your number

So someone can ring back at a more convenient time.
Thanks again for calling H. N. A.
Sláinte! Do not press zero.

Iain Crichton Smith

THOSE

Those who are given early retirement and the radiant handshake
shuffle after their wives in crowded rooms;

following them like dogs as they used to follow ideas
over horizons which were once fresh and blue.

They come to rest in fields on which once rainbows
rested like bridges among summer flowers

but now the end is in sight, the box is open
with its sweet poisons of the merciless days

and the sought fragrances which never really appear.
The hoover bites at the legs, as at great windows

they look out at the sea where boats with names
like Dayspring and Diligence rock on their rusty chains.

Tim Cumming

Suddenly he'd walk breathless into a room
or catch his breath on stairs,
at dawn, when a phone would ring,
and his heart would skip a beat.
He'd catch his clothing, or lose the key,
the plot, the sense of anything
having a recognisable purpose.
He once read a book about relaxation
and even bought a cassette
and when he slept his visions
were like the label on a bottle of good wine.
Sleep, breathlessness, and a temporary
inability to take things seriously.
The sense of having too much of everything on one plate
and the attention span of a bird's wing.
A bird caught in a smallish room.
He sat alone in his room
and hugged the phone to his chest,
counting the pips first to one hour,
and then the next.

Fred D'Aguiar

AT THE GRAVE OF THE UNKNOWN AFRICAN

1

Two round, cocoa faces, carved on whitewashed headstone
protect your grave against hellfire and brimstone.

Those cherubs with puffed cheeks, as if chewing gum,
signal how you got here and where you came from.

More than two and a half centuries after your death,
the barefaced fact that you're unnamed feels like defeat.

I got here via White Ladies Road and Black Boy's Hill,
clues lost in these lopsided stones that Henbury's vandal

helps to the ground and Henbury's conservationist
tries to rectify, cleaning the vandal's pissy love-nest.

African slave without a name, I'd call this home
by now. Would you? Your unknown soldier's tomb

stands for shipload after shipload that docked,
unloaded, watered, scrubbed, exercised and restocked

thousands more souls for sale in Bristol's port;
cab drivers speak of it all with yesterday's hurt.

The good conservationist calls it her three hundred year war;
those raids, deals, deceit and capture (a sore still raw).

St Paul's, Toxteth, Brixton, Tiger Bay and Handsworth:
petrol bombs flower in the middle of roads, a sudden growth

at the feet of police lines longer than any cricket pitch.
African slave, your namelessness is the wick and petrol mix.

Each generation catches the one fever love can't appease;
nor Molotov cocktails, nor when they embrace in a peace

far from that three-named, two-bit vandal and conservationist
binning beer cans, condoms and headstones in big puzzle-pieces.

2

Stop there black Englishman before you tell a bigger lie.
You mean me well by what you say but I can't stand idly by.

The vandal who keeps coming and does what he calls fucks
on the cool gravestones, also pillages and wrecks.

If he knew not so much my name but what happened to Africans,
he'd maybe put in an hour or two collecting his Heinekens;

like the good old conservationist, who's earned her column
inch, who you knock, who I love without knowing her name.

The dead can't write, nor can we sing (nor can most living).
Our ears (if you can call them ears) make no good listening.

Say what happened to me and countless like me, all anon.
Say it urgently. Mean times may bring back the water cannon.

I died young, but to age as a slave would have been worse.
What can you call me? Mohammed. Homer. Hannibal. Jesus.

Would it be too much to have them all? What are couples up to
when one reclines on the stones and is ridden by the other?

Will our talk excite the vandal? He woz ere, like you are now,
armed with a knife, I could see trouble on his creased brow,

love-trouble, not for some girl but for this village.
I share his love and would have let him spoil my image,

if it wasn't for his blade in the shadow of the church wall
taking me back to my capture and long sail to Bristol,

then my sale on Black Boy's Hill and disease ending my days:
I sent a rumble up to his sole; he scooted, shocked and dazed.

Here the sentence is the wait and the weight is the sentence.
I've had enough of a parish where the congregation can't sing.

Take me where the hymns sound like a fountain-washed canary,
and the beer-swilling, condom wielding vandal of Henbury,

reclines on the stones and the conservationist mounts him,
and in my crumbly ears there's only the sound of them sinning.

Sylvia Dann

Back to Nature

It's 2.00 am and after several cans
of Tennents we're getting a bit
philosophical Jim says he'll pack in
writing songs and go up the Amazon
in a canoe Mike says he fancies
lying around all day in the forest getting
pissed on jungle juice and Brendan says
that when they're all too smashed to go out
and kill a creature they'll send the
women off to gather berries they ask what
will you do I say I'll teach the women
to be assertive so they can tell you to
fuck off and pick your own berries.

Kwame Dawes

New Neighbours

and you know there is a path here
which you must find

somehow quietly
and when you find it

keep it to yourself
like a talisman

and simply toe
the line

don't
smudge it.

Michael Donaghy

My Flu

I'd swear blind it's June, 1962.
Oswald's back from Minsk. U2s glide over Cuba.
My cousin's in Saigon. My father's in bed
with my mother. I'm eight and in bed with my flu.
I'd *swear*, but I can't be recalling this sharp reek of Vicks,
the bedroom's fevered wallpaper, the neighbour's TV,
the rain, the tyres' hiss through rain, the rain smell.
This would never stand up in court – I'm asleep.

I'm curled up, shivering, fighting to wake,
but I can't turn my face from the pit in the woods
– snow filling the broken suitcases, a boy curled up,
like me, as if asleep, except he has no eyes.
One of my father's stories from the war
has got behind my face and filmed itself:
the village written off the map, its only witnesses
marched to the trees. Now all the birds fly up at once.

And who filmed *this* for us, a boy asleep in 1962
his long-forgotten room, his flu, this endless rain,
the skewed fan rattling, the shouts next door?
My fever reaches 104. But suddenly he's here,
I'd swear, all round me, his hand beneath my head
until one world rings truer than the other.

Nick Drake

IN MEMORY OF VINCENT COX
(*born Lambeth 1923, died Harpenden 1991*)

(for Iain Cox)

Who loved the knack of luck, of stakes and odds,
an ace, seven sevens, a hole in one;

who disappeared on Saturday afternoons
through the forbidden ribbon door

of the obscure betting shop, to reappear
hours later in his old leather armchair,

smiling his winnings, smoking, drinking tea
by the potful, and watching the TV.

Who loved to fly, Lancasters, a bomber's moon
on midnight raids, on Dresden in '45,

the figurine homes, churches, the platz and parks
razed, each family walking shades

where china turned to ash, and tears to salt,
glass buckled, light went blind, the phosphorus heart

crazed; who still came home against the odds
in a plane he called Mizpah ('In God we Trust').

Who traded his wings in post-war civvy street
for a wife and son, the green-belt, a salesman's car

and business travelling north to Staffordshire's
bleak pottery furnaces and crucibles;

who loved the lucent angles and singing rim
of cut-glass fluted on the blowing rod

from a bulb of light; sand, potash, lime,
oxides and carbonates, transfigured to

an affluence of decanters and services,
pastoral figures on the mantelpiece,

an attic of first editions packed in straw
for his after-life, and two porcelain

lucky angels cool in his left hand
as the right turned aces up or cast the dice.

Who watched with us on winter afternoons
the Sunday war film, equally black and white;

clipped, self-effacing, nonchalant braveries,
one engine spluttering, impossibly

homing on a wing and a prayer
to the orchestra's finale and dawn's light.

Who crash-landed in his armchair, years later,
the guilty survivor when his wife had gone

and neither luck nor prayer could win her back;
whose photograph would never speak, however

long he stared, sat in the early dark
among unwashed teacups and full ash-trays

losing the slow day's games of Patience.
Who carefully washed the cups, tidied the house,

smoked his last cigarette, pencilled a note
on the back of an envelope, and then

bailed out of the attic's small trap-door
into the hall's sudden January light.

Who played the joker, but who was not this;
the undertaker's mistaken parting

running through his hair on the wrong side,
a cotton smile on his face as if he might

rise to greet us, Lazarus at his wake,
and still believe himself to be blessed by luck.

Whom I last remember as a window ghost
in his living room reflected in the night

on an incandescent lawn of December frost,
ironing his white shirts in an empty room.

Whose older brother told a better winter's tale;
White City dog track, winter '33;

mother, the infamous gambler who seems
to have wagered and lost her husband in a bet,

was having a run of bad luck, but staked her last
(their return tube fare) in a four-dog race

on the outside track; gates up,
the inside three collide and knock each other cold,

while Outside Chance raced on under the lights
to an illuminated victory

at hopeless-to-one; which brought for Wally and Vince
a slap-up tea and a taxi home to bed.

Who was released out of a winter day,
his secrets, wishes and excuses turned to ash

while we stood in his absence, uncertain
tick-tack men signing *goodbye, goodbye*

to a lucky man who seemed to lose himself
and his laughter; a chancer of odds, grounded,

who loved to fly, the navigator
over enemy country, charts and compasses,

flight angles and lucky angels, blessed wings,
seeking the constant, simple, bright North Star

in the night sky he knew by heart.
Iain, do you remember how we'd play

for coppers or matchsticks when we were kids,
your father deftly shuffling the pack?

Who might forgive – with the grace of his good luck,
with the ghost of a chance – these words as my low stake

raised against loss and in his memory,
though I can find no words to say to you.

Jane Draycott

THE PRINCE RUPERT'S DROP

*the rapid cooling of this extraordinary glass drop
leaves it in a state of enormous tension…*

It's brilliant. It's a tear you can stand a car
on, the hard eye of a chandelier
ready to break down and cry like a baby, a rare
birth, cooled before its time. It's an ear
of glass accidentally sown in the coldest of water,
that sheer drop, rock solid except for the tail
or neck which will snap like sugar, kick like a mortar
under the surefire touch of your fingernail.

It's the pearl in a will-o'-the-wisp, the lantern asleep
in the ice, the light of St Elmo's fire in your eyes.
It's the roulette burst of a necklace, the snap
of bones in an icicle's finger, the snip of your pliers
at the neck of my heart, the fingertip working the spot
which says 'you are here' until you are suddenly not.

Carol Ann Duffy

Not a red rose or a satin heart.

I give you an onion.
It is a moon wrapped in brown paper.
It promises light
like the careful undressing of love.

Here.
It will blind you with tears
like a lover.
It will make your reflection
a wobbling photo of grief.

I am trying to be truthful.

Not a cute card or a kissogram.

I give you an onion.
Its fierce kiss will stay on your lips,
possessive and faithful
as we are,
for as long as we are.

Take it.
Its platinum loops shrink to a wedding-ring,
if you like.
Lethal.
Its scent will cling to your fingers,
cling to your knife.

Helen Dunmore

WHEN YOU'VE GOT

When you've got the plan of your life
matched to the time it will take
but you just want to press SHIFT/BREAK
and print over and over
this is not what I was after
this is not what I was after,

when you've finally stripped out the house
with its iron-cold fireplace,
its mouldings, its mortgage,
its single-skin walls
but you want to write in the plaster
"This is not what I was after,"

when you've got the rainbow-clad baby
in his state-of-the-art pushchair
but he arches his back at you
and pulps his Activity Centre
and you just want to whisper
"This is not what I was after,"

when the vacuum seethes and whines in the lounge
and the waste-disposal unit blows,
when tenners settle in your account
like snow hitting a stove,
when you get a chat from your spouse
about marriage and personal growth,

when a wino comes to sleep in your porch
on your Citizen's Charter
and you know a hostel's opening soon
but your headache's closer
and you really just want to torch
the bundle of rags and newspaper

and you'll say to the newspaper
*"This is not what we were after,
this is not what we were after."*

Douglas Dunn

FROM THE DONKEY'S EARS *(PART SIX, SECTION I)*

You haunt my poem, the way a woman should
Inhabit her husband's verses. Yes, yes,
We've put to sea. Eastern geographies
Stretch before us, part-charted on the nude

Indian Ocean, miles and miles of tears
And sweat for me, and all my sweet devoirs
Directed at imagined moon and stars
Caught in a birch branch for a hundred years.

To find a glimpse of who I am, or what,
I'll have to swallow Russia and a sea.
Each verst of water looks the same to me,
Like walking on the steppes, from one named spot

To one named spot, to one named spot, the same
And endlessly the same, an onion-steepled
Toy landmark hinting that the place is peopled,
Though only those who live there say its name

Other than tax-collectors. Here, Ocean is
Uncharted, unpoliced. It's not a 'here',
Or place. It's a nowhere. It isn't fear
Forces me say this, this big notionless

Wonder that wet space should be so spacious
Now that no land's in sight, and I'm cut free
From earth again, let loose, and this vast sea
My element, an endlessly audacious

Physics and meditation for the eye
And soul. Not fear, but welcome to such space
And welcome, welcome, to the salt no-place
Where the unbirded winds intensify

Existence to the tip of an extreme
And any time it's silent its silence is
Sinister, sudden, unexpectedness
Dwarfing all senses, an unuttered scream.

Jane Duran

GREAT GRANDFATHERS
for Henry Crompton

Sometimes you glimpse one –
a great grandfather –
among the trees
with his white hair blown forward
seated and secret,
glad to see you there
only just higher than his knees,
the checkered blanket,
sugar-line of the rivermouth
on his mouth.

You can hardly remember, later.
You were only four when he died
and neither of you in full faculties
when you met, so your greeting
was really a goodbye:
a blanket, leaves, a scrap of beard,
a river happening to a beach,
your heaven against his.

Still, when you think of him
he is tall, he is broad
as if he were set about with himself,
as if all the forests of Lancashire
had been used to build him.
He lones in his age.

His age is becoming fabulous.
Your mother says if he were alive now
he would be 102.
And there is that bundle of letters
he left behind

which you are only allowed to touch
with the delicacy of a ladybird alighting –
so brittle, so see-through.

Great, he is greater than your father,
grandfather, less great than his.
You think of going backward
like the sandpiper chasing the lost wave
wrestling with the tide
adept and forlorn
or how the balloon breath rushes back into
your mouth when you are trying
very hard to blow it up
to take to the park,
how it could blow you all the way back
right against his heart.

Paul Durcan

Just as I was dashing to catch the Dublin-Cork train,
Dashing up and down the stairs, searching my pockets,
She told me that her sister in Cork wanted a loan of the axe;
It was late June and
The buddleia tree in the backyard
Had grown out of control.
The taxi was ticking over outside in the street,
All the neighbours noticing it.
"You mean that you want me to bring her down the axe?"
"Yes, if you wouldn't mind, that is –"
"A simple saw would do the job, surely to God
She could borrow a simple saw."
"She said that she'd like the axe."
"OK. There is a Blue Cabs taxi ticking over outside
And the whole world inspecting it,
I'll bring her down the axe."
The axe – all four-and-a-half feet of it –
Was leaning up against the wall behind the settee –
The fold-up settee that doubles as a bed.
She handed the axe to me just as it was,
As neat as a newborn babe,
All in the bare buff.
You'd think she'd have swaddled it up
In something – if not a blanket, an old newspaper,
But no, not even a token hanky
Tied in a bow round its head.
I decided not to argue the toss. I kissed her goodbye.

The whole long way down to Cork
I felt uneasy. Guilt feelings.
It's a killer, this guilt.
I always feel bad leaving her
But this time it was the worst.

I could see that she was glad
To see me go away for a while,
Glad at the prospect of being
Two weeks on her own,
Two weeks of having the bed to herself,
Two weeks of not having to be pestered
By my coarse advances,
Two weeks of not having to look up from her plate
And behold me eating spaghetti with a knife and fork.
Our daughters are all grown up and gone away.
Once when she was sitting pregnant on the settee
It snapped shut with herself inside it,
But not a bother on her. I nearly died.

As the train slowed down approaching Portarlington
I overheard myself say to the passenger sitting opposite me:
"I am feeling guilty because she does not love me
As much as she used to, can you explain that?"
The passenger's eyes were on the axe on the seat beside me.
"Her sister wants a loan of the axe…"
As the train threaded itself into Portarlington
I nodded to the passenger "Cúl an tSúdaire!"
The passenger stood up, lifted down a case from the rack,
Walked out of the coach, but did not get off the train.
For the remainder of the journey, we sat alone,
The axe and I,
All the green fields running away from us,
All our daughters grown up and gone away.

U A Fanthorpe

There is a kind of love called maintenance,
Which stores the WD40 and knows when to use it;

Which checks the insurance, and doesn't forget
The milkman; which remembers to plant bulbs;

Which answers letters; which knows the way
The money goes; which deals with dentists

And Road Fund Tax and meeting trains,
And postcards to the lonely; which upholds

The permanently ricketty elaborate
Structures of living; which is Atlas.

And maintenance is the sensible side of love,
Which knows what time and weather are doing
To my brickwork; insulates my faulty wiring;
Laughs at my dryrotten jokes; remembers
My need for gloss and grouting; which keeps
My suspect edifice upright in air,
As Atlas did the sky.

Paul Farley

Funny to think you can still buy it now,
a throwback, like shoe polish or the sardine key.
When you lever the lid it opens with a sigh
and you're face-to-face with history.
By that I mean the unstable pitch black
you're careful not to spill, like mercury

that doesn't give any reflection back,
that gets between the cracks of everything
and holds together the sandstone and bricks
of our museums and art galleries;
and though those selfsame buildings stand
hosed clean now of all their gunk and soot,

feel the weight of this tin in your hand,
read its endorsement from one Abram Lyle
'Out of the strong came forth sweetness'
below the weird logo of bees in swarm
like a halo over the lion carcass.
Breathe its scent, something lost from our streets

like horseshit or coalsmoke; its base note
a building block as biblical as honey,
the last dregs of an empire's dark sump;
see how a spoonful won't let go of its past,
what the tin calls back to the mean of its lip
as you pour its contents over yourself

and smear it into every orifice.
You're history now, a captive explorer
staked out for the insects; you're tarred
and feel its caul harden. The restorer
will tap your details back out of the dark:
close-in work with a toffee hammer.

Vicki Feaver

JUDITH

Wondering how a good woman can murder
I enter the tent of Holofernes,
holding in one hand his long oiled hair
and in the other, raised above
his sleeping, wine-flushed face,
his falchion with its unsheathed
curved blade. And I feel a rush
of tenderness, a longing
to put down my weapon, to lie
sheltered and safe in a warrior's
fumey sweat, under the emerald stars
of his purple and gold canopy,
to melt like a sweet on his tongue
to nothing. And I remember the glare
of the barley field; my husband
pushing away the sponge I pressed
to his burning head; the stubble
puncturing my feet as I ran,
flinging myself on a body
that was already cooling
and stiffening; and the nights
when I lay on the roof – my emptiness
like the emptiness of a temple
with the doors kicked in; and the mornings
when I rolled in the ash of the fire
just to be touched and dirtied
by something. And I bring my blade
down on his neck – and it's easy
like slicing through fish.
And I bring it down again,
cleaving the bone.

Padraic Fiacc

Dumping (left over from the autumn)
Dead leaves, near a culvert
I come on
       a British Army soldier
With a rifle and a radio
Perched hiding. He has red hair.

He is young enough to be my weenie
- bopper daughter's boyfriend.
He is like a lonely little winter robin.

We are that close to each other, I
Can nearly hear his heart beating.

I say something bland to make him grin,
But his glass eyes look past my side
- whiskers down
         the Shore Road street.
I am an Irish man
         and he is afraid
That I have come to kill him.

Michael Foley

The best you could expect would be an answering machine:
God is attending a seminar on The Management of Change.
But to talk to the Void isn't strange. I've often prayed to stars
The distant, deaf and *non-existent* screen stars:
Marlon, share your deep power with me. Teach me to brood.
Forgive the familiar tone, Lord. I can't believe in a distant God
Who uses us for some higher purpose we can't understand
Transcendental because of a black balaclava, saying:
'This is beyond you. You'll just have to suffer. Tough turd.'
So it's casual thanks for your gifts – for Manhattan, Montmartre
And the new bridge over the Foyle that sings perpetually in the wind
Attracting a film crew in search of 'the positive aspects of Ulster life'.
I feel Godlike myself at the top of the great central span.
All you Prods to the east bank, to Deanfield, Rossbay,
                              Cedar Manor, Dunwood.
Reap your just rewards, My Chosen Ones. This Land is Your Land.
From the Waterfoot Inn to Larne Car Ferry and from Ballygawley
                              to the Giant's Causeway
Business shall flourish with the words of Isaiah on the front of the till
And no waves but in Lisnagelvin Leisure Centre new children's pool.
You Fenians, stay west in Gleneagles, Ashgrove, Baronscourt,
                              Hampstead Park.
Run up your velvet curtains there. Cast off. Lie back.
Propitious winds bear you off forever from the three-foot men
Upstream where the smoke from slacked parlour fires drifts on
                              the town
And 'the boys' fight for liberty – ('Don't do what *they* tell you.
Do what *we* tell you.') Stronger the scouring wind. Sing, bridge,
                              and fly
Your own flag – a jazzy red-and-white-striped wind sock that rides
                              high in
Untrammelled exultant wind running like beasts major corporations use
                              in their ads

The big lithe loping cats and svelte galloping thoroughbreds tossing
their manes.
Massive underfoot throb – like a great ship. Touch the rail – you feel
the singing pulse.
Extravagance and hope fill my heart. *Perhaps I won't die in Derry on a*
rainy day.
Behind me Lough Foyle and the sea, on the east the North on the west
the South
Where the statutes are frozen in stone but the statues move
And thousands churn fields to mud hoping for visions of sweet-
natured virgins.
What appears in most fields are new Tudor-style homes.
Pass on, weary traveller. Bright shine the carriage lamps, sweet
sound the chimes
But they'll bring you contempt and fury framed in wrought-iron
perms.
Here on wooded banks aluminium-framed picture windows catch
light
To make the tops of the top nested coffee tables gleam.
Money talks – wheedles, shouts, swears – but affects a sacred hush
at home.
Inward inward the gaze, blind the windows that stare on each side.
Lord, we're labelled and frozen like rich men's sperm.
Flesh is weak – and the spirit is weaker still.
Needing hard mind soft heart we loll hard of heart soft in the head.
Though we're subtle as Jesuits still when we justify.
Eastern wisdom I call my sloth and quietude.
Let the young curl their lips in contempt and my name
Be struck from the list of candidates for existential sainthood.
Lord, hear my sins. I speak as a weak man among weak men
With a heart like a deep-frozen haggis and a memory like Kurt
Waldheim.
I want to live. I want to feel. Hear me. Vouchsafe a sign.
Let me believe and care. Show me the wounds. Unclog my brain.
It's hard to remember here Your Beloved Son was a thinking man
Not the simpering half-gaga passive Sacred Heart on walls
But the fierce intense Jewish intellectual Pasolini showed

Striding up stony paths flinging truths over his shoulder
To willing but thick-headed followers stumbling behind.
Behold – a man who came not to reassure but disturb.
Awake, Fenians and Prods, from the shagpile dream of The
                                                                    Beeches
Heathfield, Summerhill, Meadowbank, Nelson Drive and Foyle
                                                                    Springs.
Come in, Daisy Hill and Mount Pleasant. Do you read me, Dunvale?
Drive if you must but leave your steamed-up cars at the picnic spots
(One at each end, the Fenian side with no rusting chassis dumped yet)
And climb to the high bracing air where great truths are revealed.
Stand above and between, look down, across and then behind
Where the untroubled Foyle spreads out grandly, inexorably.
Button car coats and ponder. The drumbeat is lost on the wind.
The blood thicker than water dissolves in the sea.
At least the vista should inspire you to country-style song:
From the Lovely Hill of Corrody to the Point of Sweet Culmore.
Sing too, new bridge – though not of what's past or passing or to come
Just the one-note song that sometimes you sing so hard in the wind
The newly social-conscious RUC have to come and close you down.
No cars stop. No one comes. Too far for the three-foot men to walk
And too many career paths here for those who want to feel Supreme.
Also it's cold. Your whole face goes numb. Who can linger on heights?
Alone, you feel more like a crank. Now the traffic grows – *both ways*.
Not a change of heart – change of shift at the chemical plant
Du Pont, just in sight to the east, seven pillars of economic wisdom
Propping up a dour sky. 'How do you find the Yanks anyway?'
'Miserable shower a shitehawks.' Yet the cars pour out eastward
Glad of the work. More leisurely the homecoming line on this side.
A typical day's freight – the sullen, the weary, the compromised.
Just a bridge, not a symbol of hope – though it sings in the wind.

Duncan Forbes

RECENSION DAY

Unburn the boat, rebuild the bridge,
Reconsecrate the sacrilege,
Unspill the milk, decry the tears,
Turn back the clock, relive the years
Replace the smoke inside the fire,
Unite fulfilment with desire,
Undo the done, gainsay the said,
Revitalise the buried dead,
Revoke the penalty and clause,
Reconstitute unwritten laws,
Repair the heart, untie the tongue,
Change faithless old to hopeful young,
Inure the body to disease
And help me to forget you please.

Matthew Francis

The Ornamental Hermit

Not really ornamental, a white figure
you might glimpse from the drive, deep in the beech woods,
as you were making your way towards the house,
standing so still he might have been a long strip
of sunlight on the bark, except that you felt,
not his eyes on you exactly, but his *thoughts*.

Hardly anyone saw him close up. The cook,
who had, said he was wearing a floppy robe
of coarse stuff and looked like a man in a bag,
and a visitor who had come face to face
with what appeared to be a nightgowned person
supposed he was mad or walking in his sleep.

No one could agree on his age. The footman
who left last night's jellied fowl and potatoes
beside his sandbank grotto in the morning
would say, after a long pause, he thought the chap
wore spectacles but he stayed in the shadows
hunched over his Bible. They were not to speak.

He was a lover who had renounced the world
or else he had been promised a thousand pounds
if he could live for seven years in the cave
that had been scooped out for him, rising at dawn,
then brooding the whole day over the hourglass,
at night praying or reading by candlelight.

Hermits were all the rage these days but this one
could not have been laid on as an ornament
for houseparties. Some of the guests went so far
as to doubt his existence, or at least claimed
that he had long ago climbed the wall, leaving
his implements in the slowly filling hole.

But it was like this. There are times when a man
must grasp where he is living. It's not enough
any more to lie under your roof at night
hearing the dry rain, to own all those acres
of dark and dirt, without someone to feel it,
to be in the thick. That's what I paid him for.

John Fuller

For my father

Considering that the world needs to be born
Endlessly out of our looking at it, it's no wonder that
We retire here for that purpose in our brief time.

Mappers and model-makers, traffickers
In language's unreliable schedules, all our
Journeying is a nostalgia for this.

The garden bears our traces and becomes
Through them the model of a mind which so
Defines itself: a part, and yet apart.

The world may grow here. All that is left outside
Is unimaginable, all within
So like itself that there is nothing else.

Blossom is rumoured. The mind also prepares
Its own best growth, pruning just beyond
The bud. Though summer is already past.

Leaves that would fly have lately fallen. Lifted
Once in wind, they have now become detached,
Ready to drift. And autumn, too, is gone.

Those purer spirits whose undeliberate music
Also creates a more or less habitual space
Have turned their retreat into a coded return.

These pebbled paths lead only to a point
Which shows where they have come from and that now
To continue is a figure not a journey.

Those walls were built no higher than they need be
And where they join give reasons for joining. Where not,
Is a hinge never still enough to cease to be one.

For to enter is always possible, as it is
To leave, though to do neither is at last
As much a relief as both were ridiculous.

If others care to overlook these long
Endeavours, let them, for after all we are
Contented merely with corroboration.

The solemnest face caught staring in would be
Your own. The reason that it never is
Seems like the reason for almost everything.

We are, possibly, posed this riddle early
In life: which is the likeliest of mirrors,
The face that reflects the world, or another face?

The last is not easily admitted, the first
The one we know. It is a grief that placed
Together they only do what mirrors do.

Reflections of reflections, it is said,
Are a symbol of all desire. And lead nowhere
But endlessly and shallow into themselves.

To see oneself in the garden is the final
Privilege, the last illusion like
The glittering letters in a burning leaf.

To be an image of the thing already
Containing you is surely a fine prospect,
As the fruit is an eager portrait of the tree.

And being so requires the greatest detachment,
Function of the philosopher's particular passion
To locate beauty beyond its short-lived shapes.

The garden, therefore, is a signal comfort
To those who fear that belonging is an illusion
Like longing itself, like the desire for desire.

For though it takes no pleasure in itself,
The garden is beautiful while you are in it,
And having once been you are always there.

Pamela Gillilan

THREE WAYS TO A SILK SHIRT

You have to kill for silk
and it's not easy. Those chrysalides
make themselves so private
in their tight shuttles, so safe
that they can dare to lose themselves
to metamorphosis, abandon the known body
and endure who can imagine what liquidity
before another form takes shape.

They must be murdered in the midst
of miracle, their cerements reeled off,
the long continuous thread saved
pliable, unstained, the severing bite
of the emerging moth forestalled.

The method's suffocation –
the oldest way by baking in hot sun;
but this hardens the thread,
makes unwinding a hard labour,
risks soiling by windborne dust,
is wasteful.

Steaming's another way – the plump bolls held
above a boiling cauldron for eight minutes
then for eight weeks spread out to dry
well-aired, so that the corpse in the shroud
desiccates slowly, leaves no stain;
but sometimes the chrysalis survives.

Surest is heated air. A single day exposed
to the technology of fans and ducts, the flow
of arid currents, and the pupa's void,
a juiceless chitin spindle shrivelled back
from the close wrappings drawn and spun
out of its former self – now to be unwound
and spun again: woven, dyed, cut and sewn,
collared and cuffed.

Chris Greenhalgh

FROM As a Matter of Fact (*Part I*)

The man sitting next to me on the plane
claimed
he'd collected one sachet of sugar
from every airline in the world.

He insisted on shaking my hand and
calling me repeatedly by my first name.
He probably has many friends and lots of money
and, feeling that exaggerated sense of mortality

you get at thirty thousand feet
and with the urge, correspondingly
strong, to relate my life-story to a stranger,
I said "no shit!" and noted parenthetically

that I had every backnumber of <u>Yeasty Catgirls</u>
ever printed, not to mention a few never
generally released. He countered with "the fact" that
he could fold a piece of paper

in half nine times. I said I'd once eaten
a whole jar of Cayenne pepper.
He rejoined that if I studied Figures 3,
7, 16 and 21 in some noted medical

encyclopaedia I'd see that the model
was him. He asked me what I did for
a living and I told him I counted cars
on a raised footbridge of the Holland Tunnel,

but that I used to be a lexicographer
with special responsibility for the letter F;
that was after I'd been a synopsiser
of detective novels. He said

he'd once appeared on CNN as a quote death-
threat recipient unquote and, as I expressed my
surprise, hostesses in British Airways livery
hovered with the suavity

of café violinists, deploying contoured
plastic laptop trays
of food on every table. Outside, the sky
griddled to pink and grey.

Lavinia Greenlaw

A World Where News Travelled Slowly

It could take from Monday to Thursday
and three horses. The ink was unstable,
the characters cramped, the paper tore where it creased.
Stained with the leather and sweat of its journey,
the envelope absorbed each climatic shift,
as well as the salt and grease of the rider
who handed it over with a four-day chance
that by now things were different and while the head
had to listen, the heart could wait.

Semaphore was invented at a time of revolution;
the judgement of swing in a vertical arm. News travelled
letter by letter, along a chain of towers, each built
within telescopic distance of the next.
The clattering mechanics of the six-shutter telegraph
still took three men with all their variables
added to those of light and weather,
to read, record and pass the message on.

Now words are faster, smaller, harder
… we're almost talking in one another's arms.
Coded and squeezed, what chance has my voice
to reach your voice unaltered and then to leave no trace?
Nets tighten across the sky and the sea bed. When London
made contact with New York, there were such fireworks
City Hall caught light. It could have burned to the ground.

Jane Griffiths

A Poem Against the Kind of Occasional Verse

which starts with a long quavering line like the run-up
to a marginal doodle on a set of lecture notes, the sort
which starts as a circle, becomes an eye, grows a quiff
and some flowers which sprout from an enormous ear
that's attached to a retrospective tea-pot spout
and culminates in a set of legs like those which belong
to an occasional table of the unassuming kind which
can always be pushed (almost) to one side: not just because
it's a way of playing consequences single-handed so even
the element of surprise is lost or because the ends of lines loiter
without intent like drunks on the pavement at closing-time but
mainly because of the pretence that the writer is simply
part of the scenery, part of a bar-stool or a swift triangle
of red skirt round the ellipse of the Sheldonian who has stumbled
upon herself as upon the occasional table or chair leg
and observed herself and written her down, unassuming
and pi as the artless voice on the telephone whispering
it's only me when really *it is I* all the time.

Thom Gunn

LAMENT

Your dying was a difficult enterprise.
First, petty things took up your energies,
The small but clustering duties of the sick,
Irritant as the cough's dry rhetoric.
Those hours of waiting for pills, shot, X-ray
Or test (while you read novels two a day)
Already with a kind of clumsy stealth
Distanced you from the habits of your health.
  In hope still, courteous still, but tired and thin,
You tried to stay the man that you had been,
Treating each symptom as a mere mishap
Without import. But then the spinal tap.
It brought a hard headache, and when night came
I heard you wake up from the same bad dream
Every half-hour with the same short cry
Of mild outrage, before immediately
Slipping into the nightmare once again
Empty of content but the drip of pain.
No respite followed: though the nightmare ceased,
Your cough grew thick and rich, its strength increased.
Four nights, and on the fifth we drove you down
To the Emergency Room. That frown, that frown:
I'd never seen such rage in you before
As when they wheeled you through the swinging door.
For you knew, rightly, they conveyed you from
Those normal pleasures of the sun's kingdom
The hedonistic body basks within
And takes for granted – summer on the skin,
Sleep without break, the moderate taste of tea
In a dry mouth. You had gone on from me
As if your body sought out martyrdom
In the far Canada of a hospital room.
Once there, you entered fully the distress

And long pale rigours of the wilderness.
A gust of morphine hid you. Back in sight
You breathed through a segmented tube, fat, white,
Jammed down your throat so that you could not speak.
   How thin the distance made you. In your cheek
One day, appeared the true shape of your bone
No longer padded. Still your mind, alone,
Explored this emptying intermediate
State for what holds and rests were hidden in it.
   You wrote us messages on a pad, amused
At one time that you had your nurse confused
Who, seeing you reconciled after four years
With your grey father, both of you in tears,
Asked if this was at last your 'special friend'
(The one you waited for until the end).
'She sings,' you wrote, 'a Philippine folk song
To wake me in the morning... It is long
And very pretty.' Grabbing at detail
To furnish this bare ledge toured by the gale,
On which you lay, bed restful as a knife,
You tried, tried hard, to make of it a life
Thick with the complicating circumstance
Your thoughts might fasten on. It had been chance
Always till now that had filled up the moment
With live specifics your hilarious comment
Discovered as it went along; and fed,
Laconic, quick, wherever it was led.
You improvised upon your own delight.
I think back to the scented summer night
We talked between our sleeping bags, below
A molten field of stars five years ago:
I was so tickled by your mind's light touch
I couldn't sleep, you made me laugh too much,
Though I was tired and begged you to leave off.

Now you were tired, and yet not tired enough
– Still hungry for the great world you were losing

Steadily in no season of your choosing –
And when at last the whole death was assured,
Drugs having failed, and when you had endured
Two weeks of an abominable constraint,
You faced it equably, without complaint,
Unwhimpering, but not at peace with it.
You'd lived as if your time was infinite:
You were not ready and not reconciled,
Feeling as uncompleted as a child
Till you had shown the world what you could do
In some ambitious role to be worked through,
A role your need for it had half-defined,
But never wholly, even in your mind.
You lacked the necessary ruthlessness,
The soaring meanness that pinpoints success.
We loved that lack of self-love, and your smile,
Rueful, at your own silliness.
                                        Meanwhile,
Your lungs collapsed, and the machine, unstrained,
Did all your breathing now. Nothing remained
But death by drowning on an inland sea
Of your own fluids, which it seemed could be
Kindly forestalled by drugs. Both could and would:
Nothing was said, everything understood,
At least by us. Your own concerns were not
Long-term, precisely, when they gave the shot
– You made local arrangements to the bed
And pulled a pillow round beside your head.
   And so you slept, and died, your skin gone grey,
Achieving your completeness, in a way.

Outdoors next day, I was dizzy from a sense
Of being ejected with some violence
From vigil in a white and distant spot
Where I was numb, into this garden plot
Too warm, too close, and not enough like pain.
I was delivered into time again

– The variations that I live among
Where your long body too used to belong
And where the still bush is minutely active.
You never thought your body was attractive,
Though others did, and yet you trusted it
And must have loved its fickleness a bit
Since it was yours and gave you what it could,
Till near the end it let you down for good,
Its blood hospitable to those guests who
Took over by betraying it into
The greatest of its inconsistencies
This difficult, tedious, painful enterprise.

Mark Halliday

WHANG EDITORIAL POLICY

The editors of *Whang* invite poetry that wears purple
stiletto heels without claiming that this is heroic,
and red football jerseys with the numeral 88.
We expect the kind of momentum and alternating current
that you'd expect with your head in the mouth of
Sophia Loren in 1957. Please single-space and leave
visible margins and italicize foreign words.
Do not assume that to say "Barcelona" or "heart of night"
or "blue soufflé" will open every door at *Whang*.
We look for poems that embrace God *because* God has failed
and not the other way around. Send only such poems
as you would choose in lieu of a cigarette before
execution by firing squad. But do not suppose
that facile verbal violence can make us gape and squirm.
We want poems that squeak with the labor of building
elastic altars, but not poems that mop and mow
upon the moony terrace, nor desiccated poems
that wring their hands above a carpet of twigs.
Strange is okay, but not So-Proud-To-Be-Odd.
If your work merely shuffles and titters
with chipmunks glimpsed teasingly in rearview mirrors,
please send it elsewhere. *Whang* is an outlet for sacred
lava. *Whang* is devoted to the nervous fingers of
the short shadowed person frowning in the bagel shop
at a book about Manhattan in the Twenties; but
this is far from the sort of poetry that is flecked
with marinara sauce and garlic amid exploding flashbulbs.
We are not complacent at *Whang*. Nor are we fixed.
We are incipient and pulsing. The world, for us,
is a vertigo of quicksand and we edit as freemasons
in the vale of Tempe, where love is only just before
the hour of quote loving unquote, and yet
your envelope won't even be opened if you think

it's merely a matter of boom image boom image boom image
boom. You have to care *more*. For us the dreamer is
a quincunx of trees in a gale of ink with a grace
as of owls that are not mere birds. For further guidelines
send nine dollars. If you are a churl, do not submit,
but do subscribe. We stay up late, and morning finds us
crusted with homage to fickle dancers whose hair is fizzy.
If you wish your poems returned, check the alley out back.
Know this, know this, we are not just "doing our thing",
we are not just "another eccentric mag". Things have gone
way, way past that. Life whispered "spring" and we sprang.
Do not take us for granted at *Whang*.

Sophie Hannah

The Mystery of the Missing

Think carefully. You sat down on a bench
and turned the pages of a small green book.
You were about to meet your friends for lunch.

> I turned the pages but I didn't look.
> It felt as if the bench was in mid-air.
> Whatever held me wouldn't put me back.

What happened next? You must have gone somewhere.
The wind was blowing hair across your face.
Perhaps you went inside and lit a fire.

> But people looked for me and found no trace
> inside or out. I saw the things they feared
> in the green book before I lost my place.

Surely they weren't afraid you'd disappeared?
Did they suspect you might have come to harm?
You could have reassured them with a word.

> I wanted to, but every word that came
> threatened to burn my mouth. I also knew
> that soon it would be over, I'd be home.

The sky closed in. You say you shrank, then grew,
then everything came back to you with ease.
You sat quite still, deciding what to do.

> Huge purple bruises covered both my knees
> But no-one acted like I'd been away.
> None of my friends asked what the matter was –

> Everyone else had had a normal day.

Mike Harding

DADDY EDGAR'S POOLS

Each week you, Thursday Millionaire, would conjure up
The ju-ju, stab the coupon with a pin
Or read the cups, perm my age and height
With Hitler's birthday and the number of
The bus that passed the window and the clump
Of pigeons on the next door neighbour's loft.

With rabbit's foot, white heather, and wishbone
You fluenced the coupon that I ran to post.

Each muggy Saturday you sat still while the set
Called out into the hushed room where I sat
With burning ears and heard a London voice
Call names as strange as shipping forecasts through the air:
Hamilton Academicals, Queen of the South,
Pontefract United, Hearts of Midlothian,
Wolverhampton Wanderers, Arbroath, Hibernian,
And once, I thought, a boy called *Patrick Thistle.*

Then every week after the final check,
When Friday's dreams were scratched out with a squeaky pen,
You took down from upstairs your brass band coat,
Gave me the wad of polish and the button stick.
And there in that still, darkened room I polished up
Each brassy button world that showed my face;
While you on shining tenor horn played out
Your Thursday Millionaire's lament
For a poor man's Saturday gone.

Tony Harrison

A Cold Coming
FROM *The Gaze of the Gorgon*

'A cold coming we had of it.'
 T S Eliot
 Journey of the Magi

I saw the charred Iraqi lean
towards me from bomb-blasted screen,

his windscreen wiper like a pen
ready to write down thoughts for men,

his windscreen wiper like a quill
he's reaching for to make his will.

I saw the charred Iraqi lean
like someone made of Plasticine

as though he'd stopped to ask the way
and this is what I heard him say:

'Don't be afraid I've picked on you
for this exclusive interview.

Isn't it your sort of poet's task
to find words for this frightening mask?

If that gadget that you've got records
words from such scorched vocal chords,

press RECORD before some dog
devours me mid-monologue.'

So I held the shaking microphone
closer to the crumbling bone:

'I read the news of three wise men
who left their sperm in nitrogen,

three foes of ours, three wise Marines
with sample flasks and magazines,

three wise soldiers from Seattle
who banked their sperm before the battle.

Did No.1 say: God be thanked
I've got my precious semen banked.

And No.2: O praise the Lord
my last best shot is safely stored.

And No.3: Praise be to God
I left my wife my frozen wad?

So if their fate was to be gassed
at least they thought their name would last,

and though cold corpses in Kuwait
they could by proxy procreate.

Excuse a skull half roast, half bone
for using such a scornful tone.

It may seem out of all proportion
but I wish I'd taken their precaution.

They seemed the masters of their fate
with wisely jarred ejaculate.

Was it a propaganda coup
to make us think they'd cracked death too,

disinformation to defeat us
with no post-mortem millilitres?

Symbolic billions in reserve
made me, for one, lose heart and nerve.

On Saddam's pay we can't afford
to go and get our semen stored.

Sad to say that such high tech's
uncommon here. We're stuck with sex.

If you can conjure up and stretch
your imagination (and not retch)

the image of me beside my wife
closely clasped creating life...

(I let the unfleshed skull unfold
a story I'd been already told,

and idly tried to calculate
the content of ejaculate:

the sperm in one ejaculation
equals the whole Iraqi nation

times, roughly, let's say, 12.5
though that .5's not now alive.

Let's say the sperms were an amount
so many times the body count,

2,500 times at least
(but let's wait till the toll's released!).

Whichever way Death seems outflanked
by one tube of cold bloblings banked.

Poor bloblings, maybe you've been blessed
with, of all fates possible, the best

according to Sophocles i.e.
'the best of fates is not to be'

a philosophy that's maybe bleak
for any but an ancient Greek

but difficult these days to escape
when spoken to by such a shape.

When you see men brought to such states
who wouldn't want that 'best of fates'

or in the world of Cruise and Scud
not go kryonic if he could,

spared the normal human doom
of having made it through the womb?)

He heard my thoughts and stopped the spool:
'I never thought life futile, fool!

Though all Hell began to drop
I never wanted life to stop.

I was filled with such a yearning
to stay in life as I was burning,

such a longing to be beside
my wife in bed before I died,

and, most, to have engendered there
a child untouched by war's despair.

So press RECORD! I want to reach
the warring nations with my speech.

Don't look away! I know it's hard
to keep regarding one so charred,

so disfigured by unfriendly fire
and think it once burned with desire.

Though fire has flayed off half my features
they once were like my fellow creatures',

till some screen-gazing crop-haired boy
from Iowa or Illinois,

equipped by ingenious technophile
put paid to my paternal smile

and made the face you see today
an armature half-patched with clay,

an icon framed, a looking glass
for devotees of "kicking ass",

a mirror that returns the gaze
of victors on their victory days

and in the end stares out the watcher
who ducks behind his headline: GOTCHA!

or behind the flag-bedecked page 1
of the true to bold-type-setting SUN!

I doubt victorious Greeks let Hector
join their feast as spoiling spectre,

and who'd want to sour the children's joy
in Iowa or Illinois

or ageing mothers overjoyed
to find their babies weren't destroyed?

But cabs beflagged with SUN front pages
don't help peace in future ages.

Stars and Stripes in sticky paws
may sow the seeds for future wars.

Each Union Jack the kids now wave
may lead them later to the grave.

But praise the Lord and raise the banner
(excuse a skull's sarcastic manner!)

Desert Rat and Desert Stormer
without scars and (maybe) trauma,

the semen-bankers are all back
to sire their children in their sack.

With seed sown straight from the sower
dump second-hand spermatozoa!

Lie that you saw me and I smiled
to see the soldier hug his child.

Lie and pretend that I excuse
my bombing by B52s,

pretend I pardon and forgive
that they still do and I don't live,

pretend they have the burnt man's blessing
and then, maybe, I'm spared confessing

that only fire burnt out the shame
of things I'd done in Saddam's name,

the deaths, the torture and the plunder
the black clouds all of us are under.

Say that I'm smiling and excuse
the Scuds we launched against the Jews.

Pretend I've got the imagination
to see the world beyond one nation.

That's your job, poet, to pretend
I want my foe to be my friend.

It's easier to find such words
for this dumb mask like baked dogturds.

So lie and say the charred man smiled
to see the soldier hug his child.

This gaping rictus once made glad
a few old hearts back in Baghdad,

hearts growing older by the minute
as each truck comes without me in it.

I've met you though, and had my say
which you've got taped. Now go away.'

I gazed at him and he gazed back
staring right through me to Iraq.

Facing the way the charred man faced
I saw the frozen phial of waste,

a test-tube frozen in the dark,
crib and Kaaba, sacred Ark,

a pilgrimage of Cross and Crescent
the chilled suspension of the Present.

Rainbows seven shades of black
curved from Kuwait back to Iraq,

and instead of gold the frozen crock's
crammed with Mankind on the rocks,

the congealed geni who won't thaw
until the World renounces War,

cold spunk meticulously jarred
never to be charrer or the charred,

a bottled Bethlehem of this come-
curdling Cruise/Scud-cursed millenium.

I went. I pressed REWIND and PLAY
and I heard the charred man say:

David Harsent

THE CURATOR

Everything under glass and still as stone. Where an item was
out on loan, a photograph gave its likeness: at a glance,
you'd own they were little but horn and bone. 'I'm busy
just now,' he said, 'why not go on alone? You can't get
easily lost. Those arrows will bring you home.'

> *This is the razor that turned on its owner,*
> *this is the finger that fired the first shot,*
> *this is the flower that poisoned its wearer,*
> *this is the riddle that started the rot.*

But when I turned the corner, he was there; of course he was.
'Aren't we a pair?' he laughed, as if climbing the stair in step,
as if breathing that mouldy air, might make us sudden
partners in Truth-or-Dare. He thumbed the catalogue; the
sheer size of it made me stare: the weight of loss. 'Is it
something particular?' As if he didn't know. 'Is it something
awry or unfair?'

> *This is the poodle that bit Aristotle,*
> *this is the tongue with the strawberry wart,*
> *this is the rattle they found in the shtetl,*
> *this is the cutie who wouldn't abort.*

He stood at the door to see me off, and wore the cloths of
frailty like the Godless poor: which fooled me not one bit.
'You've seen damn-all, you know, but if you're sure – 'He
snicked the ID off my coat and tore the lapel a token inch. 'A
souvenir...' Now I no longer wore my face and name. 'It's
queer,' he shook my hand, 'this way or that, they all come
back for more.'

This is the tumour that grew like a rumour,
this is the rafter and this is the rope,
this is the drama that buried the dreamer,
this is the hope beyond hope beyond hope.

Seamus Heaney

MYCENAE LOOKOUT

The ox is on my tongue
                    Aeschylus, *Agamemnon*

1 *The Watchman's War*
Some people wept, and not for sorrow – joy
That the king had armed and upped and sailed for Troy,
But inside me like struck sound in a gong
That killing-fest, the life-warp and world-wrong
It brought to pass, still augured and endured.
I'd dream of blood in bright webs in a ford,
Of bodies raining down like tattered meat
On top of me asleep – and me the lookout
The queen's command had posted and forgotten,
The blind spot her farsightedness relied on.
And then the ox would lurch against the gong
And deaden it and I would feel my tongue
Like the dropped gangplank of a cattle truck,
Trampled and rattled, running piss and muck,
All swimmy-trembly as the lick of fire,
A victory beacon in the abattoir . . .
Next thing then I would waken at a loss,
For all the world a sheepdog stretched in grass,
Exposed to what I knew, still honour-bound
To concentrate attention out beyond
The city and the border, on that line
Where the blaze would leap the hills when Troy had fallen.

My sentry work was fate, a home to go to,
An in-between-times that I had to row through
Year after year: when the mist would start
To lift off fields and inlets, when morning light
Would open like the grain of light being split,
Day in, day out, I'd come alive again,

Silent and sunned as an esker on a plain,
Up on my elbows, gazing, biding time
In my outpost on the roof . . . What was to come
Out of that ten years' wait that was the war
Flawed the black mirror of my frozen stare.
If a god of justice had reached down from heaven
For a strong beam to hang his scale-pans on
He would have found me tensed and ready-made.
I balanced between destiny and dread
And saw it coming, clouds bloodshot with the red
Of victory fires, the raw wound of that dawn
Igniting and erupting, bearing down
Like lava on a fleeing population . . .
Up on my elbows, head back, shutting out
The agony of Clytemnestra's love-shout
That rose through the palace like the yell of troops
Hurled by King Agamemnon from the ships.

2 *Cassandra*
No such thing
as innocent
bystanding.

Her soiled vest,
her little breasts,
her clipped, devast-

ated, scabbed
punk head,
the char-eyed

famine gawk –
she looked
camp-fucked

and simple.
People
could feel

a missed
trueness in them
focus,

a homecoming
in her dropped-wing,
half-calculating

bewilderment.
No such thing
as innocent.

Old King Cock-
of-the-Walk
was back,

King Kill-
the-Child-
and-Take-

What-Comes,
King Agamem-
non's drum-

balled, old buck's
stride was back.
And then her Greek

words came,
a lamb
at lambing time,

bleat of clair-
voyant dread,
the gene-hammer

and tread
of the roused god.
And a result-

ant shock desire
in bystanders
to do it to her

there and then.
Little rent
cunt of their guilt:

in she went
to the knife
to the killer wife,

to the net over
her and her slaver,
the Troy reaver,

saying, 'A wipe
of the sponge,
that's it.

The shadow-hinge
swings unpredict-
ably and the light's

blanked out.'

3 *His Dawn Vision*
Cities of grass. Fort walls. The dumbstruck palace.
I'd come to with the night wind on my face,

Agog, alert again, but far, far less

Focused on victory than I should have been –
Still isolated in my old disdain
Of claques who always needed to be seen

And heard as the true Argives. Mouth athletes,
Quoting the oracle and quoting dates,
Petitioning, accusing, taking votes.

No element that should have carried weight
Out of the grievous distance would translate.
Our war stalled in the pre-articulate.

The little violets' heads bowed on their stems,
The pre-dawn gossamers, all dew and scrim
And star-lace, it was more through them

I felt the beating of the huge time-wound
We lived inside. My soul wept in my hand
When I would touch them, my whole being rained

Down on myself, I saw cities of grass,
Valleys of longing, tombs, a wind-swept brightness,
And far-off, in a hilly, ominous place,

Small crowds of people watching as a man
Jumped a fresh earth-wall and another ran
Amorously, it seemed, to strike him down.

    4 *The Nights*
    They both needed to talk,
    pretending what they needed
    was my advice. Behind backs
    each one of them confided
    it was sexual overload
    every time they did it –

and indeed from the beginning
(a child could have hardly missed it)
their real life was the bed.

The king should have been told,
but who was there to tell him
if not myself? I willed them
to cease and break the hold
of my cross-purposed silence
but still kept on, all smiles
to Aegisthus every morning,
much favoured and self-loathing.
The roof was like an eardrum.

The ox's tons of dumb
inertia stood, head down
and motionless as a herm.
Atlas, watchmen's patron,
would come into my mind,
the only other one
up at all hours, ox-bowed
under his yoke of cloud
out there at the world's end.

The loft-floor where the gods
and goddesses took lovers
and made out endlessly
successfully, those thuds
and moans through the cloud cover
were wholly on his shoulders.
Sometimes I thought of us
apotheosized to boulders
called Aphrodite's Pillars.

High and low in those days
hit their stride together.
When the captains in the horse

felt Helen's hand caress
its wooden boards and belly
they nearly rode each other.
But in the end Troy's mothers
bore their brunt in alley,
bloodied cot and bed.
The war put all men mad,
horned, horsed or roof-posted,
the boasting and the bested.

My own mind was a bull-pen
where horned King Agamemnon
had stamped his weight in gold.
But when hills broke into flame
and the queen wailed on and came,
it was the king I sold.
I moved beyond bad faith:
for his bullion bars, his bonus
was a rope-net and a blood-bath.
And the peace had come upon us.

5 *His Reverie of Water*

At Troy, at Athens, what I most clearly
see and nearly smell
is the fresh water.

A filled bath, still unentered
and unstained, waiting behind housewalls
that the far cries of the butchered on the plain

keep dying into, until the hero comes
surging in incomprehensibly
to be attended to and be alone,

stripped to the skin, blood-plastered, moaning
and rocking, splashing, dozing off,
accommodated as if he were a stranger.

And the well at Athens too.
Or rather that old lifeline leading up
and down from the Acropolis

to the well itself, a set of timber steps
slatted in between the sheer cliff face
and a free-standing, covering spur of rock,

secret staircase the defenders knew
and the invaders found, where what was to be
Greek met Greek,

the ladder of the future
and the past, besieger and besieged,
the treadmill of assault

turned waterwheel, the rungs of stealth
and habit all the one
bare foot extended, searching.

And then this ladder of our own that ran
deep into a well-shaft being sunk
in broad daylight, men puddling at the source

through tawny mud, then coming back up
deeper in themselves for having been there,
like discharged soldiers testing the safe ground,

finders, keepers, seers of fresh water
in the bountiful round mouths of iron pumps
and gushing taps.

for Cynthia and Dmitri Hadzi

Stuart Henson

The Price

Sometimes it catches when the fumes rise up
among the throbbing lights of cars, or as
you look away to dodge eye-contact with
your own reflection in the carriage-glass;
or in a waiting-room a face reminds you
that the colour supplements have lied
and some have pleasure and some pay the price.
Then all the small securities you built
about your house, your desk, your calendar
are blown like straws; and momentarily,
as if a scent of ivy or the earth
had opened up a childhood door, you pause,
to take the measure of what might have been
against the kind of life you settled for.

W N Herbert

SMIRR

The leaves flick past the windows of the train
like feeding swifts: they're scooping up small mouth-
fuls of the midge-like autumn, fleeing south
with the train's hot wake: their feathers are small rain.
'Serein' they could say, where I'm passing through,
then just a sound could link rain with the leaves'
symptom, of being sere. But who deceives
themselves such rhyming leaps knit seasons now?
Some alchemist would get the point at once;
why I, against the leaves' example, try
migrating to my cold roots like a dunce.
Thicker than needles sticking to a fir,
Winter is stitching mists of words with chance,
like smears of myrrh, like our small rain, our smirr.

Selima Hill

MY LIFE WITH MEN

The first man I attracted
was my father,
who people said was young:
how young he is!
But actually he wasn't. He was old.
I told my little friends he was the lodger.
Next, the man who called me
Schlobovitz
and worshipped me unstintingly.
They all did.
And then the man I found upstairs in bed,
who said he was my
Unexpected Brother.
Why do people have to lie like that?

And later on I met his friend The Man.
And then another.
I was off my head.
I never loved them but I wanted to.
I wanted to so much I thought I did.
So much, in fact, I even married one,
and went to live in Manland, among Men;
where other women,
wrapped and stunned
like meat,
introduced me to the long machines
we mustn't leave
on pain of death
all day.

We mustn't walk,
or even go outside.
(If anyone's seen "loose" –

without a car –
they're rounded up
and given clocks and pills.)
We mustn't talk –
except, of course, effusively,
every time the phone rings.
Then we must.
(As long as what we say
is not the truth;
as long as who we're talking to's
a stranger.)

Our flowers
are dead.
Our animals
are headless.
Our children
are for smashing against walls.
And when the day
has done the best it can,
with well-scrubbed hands
we set our plastic clocks
and slip
like liners
into dreamless sleep,
remaining almost motionless till morning.

Michael Hofmann

MARVIN GAYE

He added the final 'e'
to counteract the imputation of homosexuality.
His father was plain Revd Gay, his son Marvin III.

He slept with his first hooker
in the army, coming off saltpetre.
He thought there was another word for 'virgin' that wasn't 'eunuch'.

Including duets, he had fifty-five chart entries.
His life followed the rhythm of albums and tours.
He had a 'couple of periods of longevity with a woman'.

He preached sex to the cream suits,
the halter tops and the drug-induced personality disorders.
When his hair receded, he grew a woolly hat and beard.

Success was the mother of eccentricity and withdrawal.
In Ostend he felt the eyes of the Belgians on him,
in Topanga someone cut the throats of his two Great Danes.

At forty-four, back in his parents' house,
any one of a number of Marvins might come downstairs.
A dog collar shot a purple dressing-gown, twice.

Michael Horovitz

After Browning

Summer's done
Birds in their heaven

All's well with the worm.

Louise Hudson

It Helps

They said you must talk to someone
so she talked
and talked
about the children,
schools, clothes,
about the house, garden,
car.
She talked and talked
on telephones, in pubs,
at restaurants
she'd entertain them all
with stories too scandalous
hilarious with the sound
of all those words.
She'd chat at the shops
discuss the weather, pass the time
of day, whisper about things
the children shouldn't hear;
like miscarriages, abortions,
sex or money.
At parties she could talk herself
to bed with men
make out she enjoyed it
liked them as they were.

Some nights she walked
around the house
just talking
the television murmured
upstairs the children
stirred in sleep.

It only took a split second

to slit her wrist
lengthways along the arm
they said "we didn't know
she should have said".

Ted Hughes

Flounders

Was that a happy day? From Chatham
Down at the South end of the Cape, our map
Somebody's optimistic assurance,
We set out to row. We got ourselves
Into mid-channel. The tide was flowing. We hung
Anchored. Northward-pulling, our baited leads
Bounced and bounced the bottom. For three hours –
Two or three sea-robins. Cruisers
Folded us under their bow-waves, we bobbed up,
Happy enough. But the wind
Smartened against us, and the tide turned, roughening,
Dragged seaward. We rowed. We rowed. We
Saw we weren't going to make it. We turned,
Cutting downwind for the sand-bar, beached
And wondered what next. It was there
I found a horse-shoe crab's carapace, perfect,
No bigger than a bee, in honey-pale cellophane.
No way back. But big, good America found us.
A power-boat and a pilot of no problems.
He roped our boat to his stern and with all his family
Slammed back across the channel into the wind,
The spray scything upwards, our boat behind
Twisting across the wake-boil – a hectic
Four or five minutes and he cast us off
In the lee of the land, but a mile or more
From our dock. We toiled along inshore. We came
To a back-channel, under beach-house gardens – marsh grass,
Wild, original greenery of America,
Mud-slicks and fiddler-crab warrens, as we groped
Towards the harbour. Gloom-rich water. Something
Suggested easy plenty. We lowered baits,
And out of about six feet of water
Six or seven feet from land, we pulled up flounders

Big as big plates, till all our bait had gone.
After our wind-burned, head-glitter day of emptiness,
And the slogging row for our lives, and the rescue,
Suddenly out of water easy as oil
The sea piled our boat with its surplus. And the day
Curled out of brilliant, arduous morning,
Through wind-hammered perilous afternoon,
Salt-scoured, to a storm-gold evening, a luxury
Of rowing among the dream-yachts of the rich
Lolling at anchor off the play-world pier.

How tiny an adventure
To stay so monumental in our marriage,
A slight ordeal of all that might be,
And a small thrill-breath of what many live by,
And a small prize, a toy miniature
Of the life that might have bonded us
Into a single animal, a single soul –

It was a visit from the goddess, the beauty
Who was poetry's sister – she had come
To tell poetry she was spoiling us.
Poetry listened, maybe, but we heard nothing
And poetry did not tell us. And we
Only did what poetry told us to do.

Kathleen Jamie

Forget It

History in a new scheme. I stretch
through hip, ribs, oxter, bursting
the cuff of my school shirt, because
this, Mr Hanning, is me.
'Sir! Sir! Sir!
– he turns, and I claim
just one of these stories,
razed places, important as castles,
as my own. *Mum!*

We done the slums today!
I bawled from the glass
front door she'd long desired.
What for? bangs the oven shut,
Some history's better forgot.
                    So how come
we remember the years
before we were born? Gutters
still pocked with fifties rain,
trains cruised dim
street-lit afternoons; war
at our backs. The black door
of the close wheezed
till you turned the third stair
then resounded like cannon.
A tower of bannisters. Nana
and me toiled past windows
smeared in blackout, condemned
empty stone. The neighbours had flitted
to council-schemes, or disappeared. . .

Who were the disappeared? Whose
the cut-throat

razor on the mantelpiece, what man's
coat hung thick with town gas, coal
in the lobby press?
                    And I mind
being stood, washed like a dog
with kettle and one cold tap
in a sink plumbed sheer
from the window
to the back midden
as multistoreys rose
across the goods yard,
and shunters clanked
through nights shared
in the kitchen recess bed.

I dreamed about my sister in America
I doot she's dead. What rural
feyness this? Another sibling
lost in Atlantic cloud,
a hint of sea in the rain –
the married in England,
the drunken and the mad,
a couple of notes postmarked Canada,
then mist: but this is a past
not yet done, else how come
our parents slam shut, deny
like criminals: *I can't remember, cannae*
mind, then turn at bay: *Why?*

Who wants to know? Stories
spoken through the mouths
of closes: who cares
who trudged those worn stairs,
or played in now rubbled back greens?
What happened about my granddad? Why
did Agnes go? How come
you don't know

that stories are balm,
ease their own pain, contain
a beginning, a middle –
and ours is a long driech
now-demolished street. *Forget it!*
Forget them that vanished,
voted with their feet,
away for good
or ill through the black door
even before the great clearance came,
turning tenements outside-in,
exposing gas pipes, hearths
in damaged gables, wallpaper
hanging limp and stained
in the shaming rain.

History, Mr Hanning.
The garden shrank for winter,
and mum stirred our spaghetti hoops
not long before she started back
part-time at Debenhams
to save for Christmas,
the odd wee
luxury, our first
foreign
holiday.

Alan Jenkins

MISSING

Messages. The dumb machine's small bright red eye
is blinking on and off, and I'm home and dry –
the cat uncurls and looks up, stretching, yawning
in a wedge of light between the windowsill and broken
   blind,
the grey-blue light of five-thirty in the morning...
The blue light was my blues, the red light was my mind...
Another half an hour and the adult video begins
once more behind my bloodshot, sleepless eyes:
is it life-saving, wrestling? Everybody wins, she pushes him away
but only to clutch him closer, surprise, surprise,
no dream-stewardess is offering me coffee, though it's day
coming red-eyed over the roofs, over the rim
of the world, bringing for me cat's-breath, for her: him.

                              *

Under-achieving, Underground-haunting, I descended to
a twilit flickering world, as I'd been led to expect;
I followed with my eyes the lighted windows rattling past
and found you out in one of them, moving too fast
for a sound to leave my open mouth. Could I detect
some sadness on your face, beautiful, downcast?
What assignation drew you on? There came a blast
of noise, a rush of foul air, a red light changed to green
somewhere far down the line, you did not look back,
and in your hurry to be moving you had not seen
how in another second you'd be changing track...
If you are Eurydice, could I be Orpheus, I mean
could anything I might still say or sing reclaim you?

                              *

Return, re-run, a dream of moon-reflecting sea,
a neon beach-bar, teenage crowd and glowing jukebox,
the screen alive with ghosts, the comical dubbed voices
and the couples sitting, knees drawn up on the sand;

we are drifting away from them, close and slow,
not talking, arms around each other's shoulders lightly –
the whole day's heat has soaked into our itching backs…
We kiss, your tongue is warm and quick, but something stops you,
you break away and run towards the sea, you turn and
suddenly, remembering *It's not like years ago*
the fear of getting caught   the recklessness in water
a flash of white your little gasp and you are swimming brightly
away from me   the undertow   *What if there were two*

*

Paris, and the boulevard I walked down with you
towards your mother's charming attic, your mother who
so charmingly stayed with friends while we played house
and fooled around; and here is the café where you sat
for you to take your picture, pouting *à la parisienne*;
here is the little bridge that crosses to the Ile St Louis
where you clutched me – though we were already late
for our rendezvous, for the movie, everything –
and opened your lips and said 'Kiss me! On ze mouse!';
here are the old men by their bookstalls, regarding me strangely
for here I am weeping, remembering *St Louis. Louis*, the Seine
cold-grey below, staring until one of them takes my arm
gently, and leads me nowhere, away from here, from harm.

*

Heroine of your teen romance, and so much a child
that when I called and found you swaddled on a sofa
in a kind of nappy (the 'thing' had split, you'd been emptied out
and the blood and after-pain were all you had to suffer)
you could smile at me, a dazed and happy smile
as I fed you cakes and poured champagne – sweet things…
We were celebrating, I was yours – why should you doubt? –
and had been since the night you shyly asked to stay,
unpeeled, unhooked, turned unhesitatingly
towards me, 'trembling with excitement' as you later said;
no thought for the thing flushed down, away,
no thought for the world that wasn't you and me,
no thought, now, for me (sweet things he told you 'turned your head').

You were quiet, in your bath, and you were going to sleep with him.
I knew it, the cat knew it. The bath-water felt it,
and the sliver of soap with which you soaped your quim,
the sponge with which you soaked your breasts, both smelt it –
when you clasped your nose and swiftly ducked
(sink or swim, you witch!) your hair waved like sea-grass,
your thatch, laid flat like tangled seaweed, foam-flecked,
lifted on the swell, and a slither of eel-slick skin
showed like the pearl-pink inside of a shell…
You surfaced, shifted slightly, settled your arse.
I saw it clenching tightly as his fingers gripped,
I saw your sea-anemone open, close as he plunged in.
Looking up, you smiled. I would say you slipped.

*

She moves on. She moves on,
taking with her when she's gone
your jacket, jeans and shirts,
your better self. It hurts and hurts.

She moves on. 'What this place needs',
she said when she first stayed the night,
'is a woman's touch.'
And she gave it that all right –
books trashed, clogged hairs in the sink;
she scarred your back, kneed you in the crotch,
told you that you stank of drink,
stabbed you in the heart. It bleeds and bleeds.

She moves on. Into another world,
one in which you don't belong
and one in which she never furled
her legs round yours, and the song
has changed, for ever, and is wrong:
not 'Marry me' or 'Let's do it'
but 'I want us to be friends.'
And you can see right through it,

and it claws and claws, and never ends.

She moves on. Now what she thinks
is that you didn't love her, not enough,
and that he's 'easy-going'. And it's tough,
your wanting her. It stinks.

She moves on. She doesn't call,
she won't come back, she's too far in,
her love was as fake as her leopardskin,
as quickly shed. You fall and fall.

She moves on. Like a single cell,
like a virus, with as much in mind,
as much concern for what it leaves behind,
as much speed. And it's hell, it's hell.

*

Missing, believed lost, five feet four-and-a-half
of warm girl, of freckled skin and sulky laugh
and blood on the sheets and ash on the pillow
with the smell of bacon eggs and lubricant – how that lingers –
for breakfast; crumpled things to scoop up from the floor and press
against my face, and cunt-smell on my fingers;
I'll skip the part about love it seems so silly and low
– the aftertaste of afternoons in a strange bed in a stranger's
flat, 'I love the way you go down on me', breathless, 'more.
Harder', and a red dress from the wardrobe, and the dangers:
at 3 a.m. your boot like a bad dream pounding on the door
and the way that anything you wanted could be true,
if you said it was. But not this. Missing. You.

*

Over. It's over. Three words uttered matter-of-factly
that I hear over and over in the sound of the wheels
hissing through rain, pointed north, as I drift in and of sleep
on the back seat, remembering our scenes, line by line, exactly
remembering line by line the words that tell you how it feels
to have brought this sadness with you from the womb

remembering *I could turn you inside out* on the car stereo
you swung like a handbag to our hotel room
and your body kneeling, bent double, face buried in the duvet,
 remembering how I stayed awake all night to watch you sleep,
lips parted, eyelids flickering *She is so beautiful she is so young*
   and Oh
our drive next day through driving rain, our bickering
I can't stand this, give me 'Les douleurs', give me Dufay

*

Viera Lodge: a drystone wall and one bent tree
and nothing else between us and the boiling sea,
the slate-grey, roiling sea. The wind wails
and we are safe inside, drinking, hearing how
a boy from the island, nineteen, hanged himself for love
of a girl up for the holidays from Glasgow.
And suddenly, for no reason, or for love,
I see myself walking down the slight slope of lawn
in the awful slate-grey light of dawn,
the cat prowling round an empty flat, listening for the key
in the lock, racing after shadows; red sails
in the sunset, a profile in the prow – it's you –
a world away from where I lie, bloated, blue.

*

Every move you make, every step you take – the 'disco-deck'
throbs, a blaze of glory as the evening flashes, fades;
waterlight flushes us, glass after glass brings back the blood
to day-defeated faces, each one doing its best
to hide a grey fatigue. You are not here, we flash and fade
as the loud, lit boat glides through London, I am obsessed –
in a small saloon, a scattering of couples watch the end
of *L'Atalante*, then *Ai No Corrida*, cries and whispers drowned
by the throbbing engine. You saw it with a girlfriend
and called to say, 'I need you, now. Can I come round?' –
I turned you away. My stomach churns, I turn and wade through dreck
of bodies – every vow you break, every smile you fake –
that twist and writhe in water, clutch and clasp in mud.

*

She came racing towards me, across a dancefloor
littered with tables, bottles, petals; she wore a flower
behind her ear, her hair piled high on her head,
wisps falling carelessly; my child-bride, my sweet
stamped her foot, one side then the other, flamenco-style,
gathered her skirt in both hands, by the hem,
and tugged it, left, right, in time with her stamping feet;
raced towards me, zig-zagged, in front of me, behind,
a challenge in her eyes and in her wide white smile...
It's crazy what you could have had, it's crazy what you could have had,
it seems a shame to waste your time to me – R.E.M.
remind me, I re-wind, replay, I know by heart
that was just a dream Pause Stop *I need this* Start

*

Now that I no longer sleep,
now I could no more count sheep
than the nights they spend together, or apart,
now I pray she'll have a heart
and come back, and come back,
now I stare into a black
and featureless night that goes on
and on, a grey and featureless dawn,
now that the telephone is quiet
and the memory runs riot,
now that I mix up the days
and am fuck-all use in several ways,
now that she's safely in the sack
with someone else, and won't come back,
now that I'm rotted through and stink
of loneliness, self-pity, drink,
now that she's finally taken off
and I'm left here to shake and cough
and wait for my first heart-attack
or for her to wake up and come back,
now that no-one wants to know
who I see, what I do or where I go,
now that more flee from me each week,

the women who sometime did me seek,
than I've had dinners on my plate,
now that her love has turned to hate
I think of this: the open-handed way I had
of slapping her, her lovely face, her head,
and making her see stars,
or pushing her downstairs
and out of the door. There's more –

*

Open me, the book says – *Cherokee*, by Jean Echenoz –
when I brush it, hunting up something else, and so I do,
and on the title-page, an entry-wound, black and yellow-brown,
the words 'Hole by Murphy, summer 1991' –
the ash dropped from your cigarette, your head dropped in a doze
to your chest, and the paper burned right through
to page thirteen; the sun in Brittany burned down,
your head jerked upright from its dream, your face was flushed
and freckled, your plump pale arms and shoulders turning red –
had your mother seen, your aunt seen? They went on sipping tea
and talking. Was it that day you wrote 'Nom d'une pipe,
tu me manques' and sent the postcard that flutters now from the book
you gave back sheepishly, unread? (Tearstains by Alan, 1993)

*

Night, the roof is leaking, and I perform my dance
with saucepan and bucket, and the steady drip, drip
of dirty water tells how love leaked out of my life;
for two years, I tried to stop the holes and fill the cracks
but there were always more, and the slow drip of slights,
insults, screaming on the telephone, hanks of hair
yanked out, left a stain that spread everywhere.
So now that the roof leaks, and the cat looks askance
at my attempts to catch as I would a second chance
these drops like huge tears falling from black heights,
I drink up regret, to the last drop,
and stop and let it all come down in cataracts
to drown me: night and rain and the thought of my not-wife.

Fred Johnston

MUSIC
for Máirtín O Connor

We talk about it in some fashion
every time we meet
the characteristics of the Irish psyche
low-hung weather like muslin over the eyes
a tendency to think too much about ourselves
and what this sun-lack does to poetry

a grainy drift of history
moves over the pier at Annaghdown
Raftery's sung dead under the blowy water
the note wind makes on the lip of a reed
the shape of music working in the bone –
the sacrament of dreaming turned to sound.

Jenny Joseph

In your honour I have cleaned the windows
Of four-months' sorrow-flung obscuration and dirt
And cut my hair and thrown away old rags
That make cupboards foetid, suffused with miserly pain.
I shall wipe the mould out of the corners
Rub down, prepare to paint;   in your honour.

And in your honour
Am throwing out old nastiness with the floorboards,
Memories of hurt, *lèse majesté*
Along with the shards and glue, useless and hard now.

As if for new love turning a new leaf over
I will pick off infestation up to the minute.
At this time of budding give a chance to cleanliness
Make beds freshly in garden, and in the house
Fresh covers; as if with hope square corners
In expectation, in honour of your coming.

For your comfort and in your honour
I have laid by stores and funds of robustness
Sweeping despondence out with the spiders' coatings
Disinfecting anxiety, self-pity
The damp that clads, sours and eats the woodwork.

I think it isn't true that ghosts return
Only to ruins and to broken things.
Shy visitants that start to come with me
Along the track I make you from the past
By thinking of you, you would never bear
Burdens you could not shoulder when alive.
You'll still want cheering, self-reliance, comfort
The big wheel pulling up the hill, hearth cleared,

Coal ordered, landlord dealt with, 'sociables',
And so to welcome you and keep a place
For your reviving influence to bide in
I move within the chrysalis of doubt
Wound round for Winter comfort, for survival.

In honour of love, in hope of expectation
I leave behind drab covering that kept me
Safe through the Winter, safe and solitary.

The grub without its carapace is needed
Pale and soft and vulnerable, for birds
Shining and voracious.   So,
I am persuaded, every time a fool.
Well, something must feed the remorselessness of Spring.

The skin will burst, so you should see light wings
No dirty brown slough. The bad times swept away,
Place ready for the prodigal,
                                              and be damned the peril
The piercing light and the brief high flight will bring.

Ashes, when you have gone, burnt bits on the lamp
That lit you on your way, but in your honour
As you pass by the window, love – bright flame.

Jackie Kay

CHAPTER 7: BLACK BOTTOM

Maybe that's why I don't like
all this talk about her being black,
I brought her up as my own
as I would any other child
colour matters to the nutters;
but she says my daughter says
it matters to her

I suppose there would have been things
I couldn't understand with any child,
we knew she was coloured.
They told us they had no babies at first
and I chanced it didn't matter what colour it was
and they said *oh well are you sure
in that case we have a baby for you* –
to think she wasn't even thought of as a baby,
my baby, my baby

I chase his *Sambo Sambo* all the way from the school gate.
A fistful of anorak – What did you call me? Say that again.
Sam-bo. He plays the word like a bouncing ball
but his eyes move fast as ping pong.
I shove him up against the wall,
say that again you wee shite. *Sambo, sambo,* he's crying now

I knee him in the balls. What was that?
My fist is steel; I punch and punch his gut.
Sorry I didn't hear you? His tears drip like wax.
Nothing he heaves *I didn't say nothing*.
I let him go. He is a rat running. He turns
and shouts *Dirty Darkie* I chase him again.
Blonde hairs in my hand. Excuse me!
This teacher from primary 7 stops us.
Names? I'll report you to the headmaster tomorrow.
But Miss. Save it for Mr Thompson she says

My teacher's face cracks into a thin smile
Her long nails scratch the note well well
I see you were fighting yesterday, again.
In a few years time you'll be a juvenile delinquent.
Do you know what that is? Look it up in the dictionary.
She spells each letter with slow pleasure.
Read it out to the class.
Thug. Vandal. Hooligan. Speak up. Have you lost your tongue?

To be honest I hardly ever think about it
except if something happens, you know
daft talk about darkies. Racialism.
Mothers ringing my bell with their kids
crying *You tell. You tell. You tell.*
– *No.* You tell your little girl to stop calling
my little girl names and I'll tell my little girl
to stop giving your little girl a doing.

We're practising for the school show
I'm trying to do the Cha Cha and the Black Bottom
but I can't get the steps right
my right foot's left and my left foot's right
my teacher shouts from the bottom
of the class Come on, show

us what you can do I thought
you people had it in your blood.
My skin is hot as burning coal
like that time she said Darkies are like coal
in front of the whole class – my blood
what does she mean? I thought

she'd stopped all that after the last time
my dad talked to her on parents' night
the other kids are all right till she starts;
my feet step out of time, my heart starts
to miss beats like when I can't sleep at night –
What Is In My Blood? The bell rings, it is time.

Sometimes it is hard to know what to say
that will comfort. Us two in the armchair;
me holding her breath, 'they're ignorant
let's have some tea and cake, forget them'.

Maybe it's really Bette Davis I want
to be the good twin or even better the bad
one or a nanny who drowns a baby in a bath.
I'm not sure maybe I'd prefer Katharine
Hepburn tossing my red hair, having a hot
temper. I says to my teacher Can't I be
Elizabeth Taylor, drunk and fat and she
just laughed, not much chance of that.
I went for an audition for the *The Prime*
of Miss Jean Brodie. I didn't get a part
even though I've been acting longer
than Beverley Innes. So I have. Honest.

Olubayo was the colour of peat
when we walked out heads turned
like horses, folk stood like trees
their eyes fixed on us – it made me
burn, that hot glare; my hand
would sweat down to his bone.
Finally, alone, we'd melt
nothing, nothing would matter

He never saw her. I looked for him in her;
for a second it was as if he was there
in that glass cot looking back through her.

On my bedroom wall is a big poster
of Angela Davis who is in prison
right now for nothing at all
except she wouldn't put up with stuff.
My mum says she is *only* 26
which seems really old to me
but my mum says it is young
just imagine, she says, being on
America's Ten Most Wanted People's List at 26!
I can't.
Angela Davis is the only female person
I've seen (except for a nurse on TV)
who looks like me. She had big hair like mine
that grows out instead of down.
My mum says it's called an *Afro*.
If I could be as brave as her when I get older
I'll be OK.

Last night I kissed her goodnight again
and wondered if she could feel the kisses
in prison all the way from Scotland.
Her skin is the same too you know.
I can see my skin is that colour
but most of the time I forget,
so sometimes when I look in the mirror
I give myself a bit of a shock
and say to myself *Do you really look like this?*
as if I'm somebody else. I wonder if she does that.

I don't believe she killed anybody.
It is all a load of phoney lies.
My dad says it's a set up.
I asked him if she'll get the electric chair
like them Roseberries he was telling me about.
No he says the world is on her side.
Well how come she's in there then I thinks.
I worry she's going to get the chair.
I worry she's worrying about the chair.
My dad says she'll be putting on a brave face.
He brought me a badge home which I wore
to school. It says FREE ANGELA DAVIS.
And all my pals says 'Who's she?'

Mimi Khalvati

STONE OF PATIENCE

'In the old days,' she explained to a grandchild bred in England,
'in the old days in Persia, it was the custom to have a stone,
a special stone you would choose from a rosebed, or a goat-patch,
a stone of your own to talk to, tell your troubles to,
a stone we called, as they now call me, a stone of patience.'

No therapists then to field a question with another,
but stones from dust where ladies' fingers, cucumbers
curled in sun. Were the ones they used for gherkins
babies that would have grown, like piano tunes had we known
the bass beyond the first few bars? Or miniatures?

Some things I'm content to guess: colour in a calyx-tip,
is it gold or mauve? A girl or a boy... Patience
was so simple then: waiting for the clematis to open,
to purple on a wall; the bud to shoot out stamens,
the jet of milk to leave its rim like honey

on the bee's fur. But patience when the cave is sealed,
a boulder at the door, is riled by the scent of hyacinth
in the blue behind the stone: the willow by the pool
where once she sat to trim a beard with kitchen scissors,
to tilt her hat at smiles, at sleep, at congratulations.

And a woman, faced with a lover grabbing for his shoes
when women-friends would have put themselves in hers,
no longer knows what's virtuous. Will anger shift
the boulder, buy her freedom, and the earth's? Or patience,
like the earth's, be abused? Even nonchalance

can lead to courage, to conception: a voice that says
oh come on darling, it'll be all right, oh do let's.
How many children were born from words such as these?
I know my own were; now learning to repeat them, to outgrow
a mother's awe of consequences her body bears.

So now that midsummer, changing shape, has brought in
another season, the grape becoming raisin, hinting
in a nip at the sweetness of a clutch, one fast upon another;
now that the breeze is raising sighs from sheets
as she tries to learn again, this time for herself.

to fling caution to the winds like colour in a woman's skirt
or to borrow patience from the stones in her own backyard
where fruit still hangs on someone else's branch... don't ask her
whose? as if it mattered. Say: *they won't mind*
as you reach for a leaf, for the branch, and pull it down.

August Kleinzahler

SUNDAY MORNING

How oddly content, these dogs of the homeless,
asleep at their feet in doorways, under benches,
good, healthy coats, breathing easily

Sunday morning in the fog downtown, in the quiet
as the hotels and neighborhoods awaken
to clouds of eggs and excrement, the chatter

on color TVs, spectacular reds and greens.
The ragged sleepers tremble under blankets
of newsprint, cough, turn over, curl as far

into themselves as they can, careening through
the switchbacks of dreams, fighting the wheel
as they barrel downhill, working that clutch

till the brakes go... *Oh*, with a muffled cry,
suddenly in the world like newborn babes,
except on Market, filthy and cold.

The dog opens one eye, no trouble, old routine.
Sighs and dozes off again, snoring
a thin wheezing snore, muzzle to sidewalk.

He is a well-looked-after animal,
fed as best as one can, touched, held.
The man tickles behind his dog's ear.

Fella's ear twitches. He calls him *Fella*.
That's what the guy he got him off called him.
Good, brown, short-haired mutt,

not too dumb and doesn't make a big fuss.
All of his pleasure, all that's left of love –
ridiculous tragic: 45lbs. of snoring dog.

But it's mutual, you see, and genuine.
Real as warm food in an empty belly.
And, in fact, that's just what it is for them both:

Fella's dog smell, the heat that raises it,
and that sour, musty smell the man has,
they all have, the stairwells and walls have

wherever they congregate. But Fella's friend
has his very own, very delicious smell,
a bit like old bones, urine, soup.

Frank Kuppner

FROM LAST ETERNAL MOMENTS (*SECTION* 76)

Some think God tortures us because he loves us so much.
What a shame he does not hate us, and treat us kindly.
Thus: every evening, regularly, for six or seven years,
The inoffensive and devout middle-aged woman
Lights a candle in front of a favoured religious image,
And prays intently. I do not know what for,
But it was not for this. One night, the candle
Catches the hem of her highly flammable nightdress,
Envelops her in flames, and burns her to death.
Thus she is taken off to meet her God of Love,
Possibly with a ready question on her lips.
Let us hope he was wearing some means of identification.
He could so easily be mistaken for his opposite number
By anyone who judges character in the light of actions.

Linton Kwesi Johnson

MI REVALUESHANARY FREN

mi revalueshanary fren is nat di same agen
yu know fram wen?
fram di masses shatta silence –
staat fi grumble
fram pawty paramoncy tek a tumble
fram Hungary to Poelan to Romania
fram di cozy cyaasle dem staat fi crumble
wen wi buck-up wananada in a reaznin
mi fren always en up pan di same ting
dis is di sang im love fi sing:

Kaydar e ad to go
Zhivkov e ad to go
Husak e ad to go
Honnicka e ad to go
Chowcheskhu e ad to go
jus like apartied
will av to go

awhile agoh mi fren an mi woz taakin
soh mi seh to im:

wat a way di eart a run nowadays, man
it gettin aadah by di day
fi know whey yu stan
cauz wen yu tink yu deh pan salid dry lan
wen yu teck a stack yu fine yu ina quick-san
yu noh notice ow di lanscape a shiff
is like valcanoe andah it an notn cyaan stap it
cauz tings jusa bubble an a bwoil doun below
strata sepahrate an refole

an wen yu tink yu reach di mountain tap
is a bran-new platow yu goh buck-up

mi revalueshanary fren shake im ed an im sigh
dis woz im reply:

Kaydar e ad to go
Zhivkov e ad to go
Husak e ad to go
Honnicka e ad to go
Chowcheskhu e ad to go
jus like apartied
will av to go

well mi nevah did satisfy wid wat me fren mek reply
an fi get a deepa meanin in di reaznin
mi seh to im:

well awrite
soh Garby gi di people dem glashnas
an it poze di Stallinist dem plenty prablem
soh Garby leggo peristrika pan dem
canfoundin bureacratic strategems
but wi haffi face up to di cole facks
im also open up pandora's bax
yes, people powa jus a showa evry howa
an evrybady claim dem demacratic
but some a wolf an some a sheep
an dat is prablematic
noh tings like dat yu woulda call dialectic?

mi revalueshanary fren pauz awhile an im smile
den im look mi in mi eye an reply:

Kaydar e ad to go
Zhivkov e ad to go
Husak e ad to go
Honnicka e ad to go
Chowcheskhu e ad to go
jus like apartied
will av to go

well mi couldn elabarate
plus it woz gettin kinda late
soh in spite a mi lack af andahstandin
bout di meanin a di changes
in di east fi di wes, nonediless
an alldow mi av mi rezahvaeshans
bout di cansiquenses an implicaeshans
espehshally fi black libahraeshan
to bring di reaznin to a canclueshan
ah ad woz to agree wid mi fren
hopein dat wen wi meet up wance agen
wi coulda av a more fulla canvahsaeshan

soh mi seh to im, yu know wat?
im seh wat? mi seh:

Kaydar e ad to go
Zhivkov e ad to go
Husak e ad to go
Honnicka e ad to go
Chowcheskhu e ad to go
jus like apartied
soon gaan

James Lasdun

EDEN

Winter, nighttime, Jane Street and West Fourth,
Three blocks east of the Hudson, brownstones
    trussed
In garters of lacy black wrought iron,
Steam-spooks and gravelled moonlight, frost...

It might have been the second night of creation;
Stellar silence, a triple-locked
Empty universe waiting for the first spoor
To lug its baggage five flights to the door –

For two days I didn't unpack.
I liked the ringing air distilled
Out of bare walls and empty shelves,
The whiff of promise not yet unfulfilled,

I could be anyone; I bought three vast
Elaborate tropical stems – a token
Of the man I was to become:
Freed, flamboyant, bigger-hearted...

I watched a tongue unfurl, fanned ganglia,
Dewlaps, a clutch of hatching parakeets
The room swarmed in a puce light –
I couldn't wait for them to die;

It seemed they never would: the coil and bloom
Convulsive, intimate; a masque of carnage –
Adam, Eve and Lilith, one stem each,
As if they'd sprouted from my own flesh.

In June the prehistoric gingkos
Swam veinless leaves through the greased, sizzling air,
We lay in the emerald swamplight
Listening to the monkey yelp of sirens –

Dawn was the dawn of time: Triceratops
Hauled its meat off the screen at Naturemax
And rumbled down Columbus.
I woke to hear it snuffling in the garbage.

Michael Laskey

HOME MOVIES

By the final frame of the film, before
the tinny rattle of a jerked reel
or that dazzle on the bald sitting-room wall,
Dad had leaped up beside the projector

and flicked the switch, so their shaky story
went ratcheting on, only backwards now:
led in by balloons, bouncing cans and clouds
of exhaust, the car came reversing surely

far too fast at the horseshoe of guests
crowding Gran's gravel, and we had to laugh
at the way our would-be father muffed
his entrance, emerging bottom first

to pose for a moment with his right arm
flung round an untarnished version of Mum.
No sound, just a pan of everyone
cracking up, the storm before the calm

delivery by Dad of some old joke.
Hilarious how they all skedaddled
backwards up the steps into the middle
of the reception: a piece of cake

that a waitress snatched; each hopeful wish
promptly returning unopened to sender
as the knife they were forcing up together
lifted off, leaving the icing unblemished;

a quick balancing trick put the tiers in place;
then unedited longueurs – little movement,
too many self-conscious close-ups of distant
relations and friends they'd lost without trace

and whom we'd never known – nothing comical
except for a slim-line uncle Jim
brightening as glass after glass of his wine
vanished, sucked up by the mouth of the bottle.

It was round about then, while we were all
full of it, paralytic at him
sobering up, that Mum left the room
with a kind of abruptness that niggled

(or would have, if we'd adjusted our focus,
not chosen not to notice) and so she missed
what followed: their ceremonial kiss
outside the church; Dad reaching across

to conceal her face with the antique veil;
and once the blinking guests had withdrawn
into the dark doorway arm in arm
he steered her backwards, helped by two small

bridesmaids tugging her train in towards
the vestry, the moment when he'd unscrew
his pen and one by one they'd undo
their signatures, going over the words

from right to left so they disappeared,
and suddenly the twinkle in Dad's eye
was a hard gleam in the flickering light
and the rare warmth of the atmosphere

too close: not one of us raised the ghost
of a laugh as Dad softly eased the ring
off the finger so gladly held out to him,
or dared interrupt to point out the past

was spilling out, already ankle-deep
on the floor and spreading. He stood so still
we didn't exist. There was nothing real
but that slither of negatives at his feet.

John Levett

A Shrunken Head

He's been stitched-up; two gummed, black-threaded eyes
Squint back across the decades in surprise
Through spiteful chinks of sunlight, acrid smoke,
Screwed-up against some wicked tribal joke.
His rictus has been sewn into a smile,
A tight-lipped dandy, puckered into style,
The clearing where his grisly fame began
Still broods beneath the kinks of wood-stained tan.
Flayed leather now, his features smoked and cured,
His niche in culture gruesomely secured,
The needled grin is fixed, drawn back and set
Bone-dry in its reflective cabinet.
A hundred years ago he strayed alone
Towards this room of ritual skin and bone,
Believed in spirits, drank, was secretive
With knives and fish-hooks, dreamed his seed would live,
Sheathed his penis, sweated half the night
On invocations, prayed, prepared to fight,
And felt, perhaps, the moon's leaf-parted shine
Move up his legs and bathe his severed spine;
His head hacked off, half-baked into this face
That swings and grins inside its airless case.
Hung-up, he seems to twitch at each dropped word,
As if, although we whisper, he had heard,
And stares through us to what we cannot see,
Our unstitched smiles, their pale atrocity.

Gwyneth Lewis

Welsh was the mother tongue, English was his.
He taught her the body by fetishist quiz,
father and daughter on the bottom stair:
'Dy benelin yw *elbow*, dy wallt di yw *hair*,

chin yw dy ên di, *head* yw dy ben.'
She promptly forgot, made him do it again.
Then he folded her *dwrn* and, calling it fist,
held it to show her knuckles and wrist.

'Let's keep it from Mam, as a special surprise.
Lips are *gwefusau*, *llygaid* are eyes.'
Each part he touched in their secret game
thrilled as she whispered its English name.

The mother was livid when she was told.
'We agreed, no English till four years old!'
She listened upstairs, her head in a whirl.
Was it such a bad thing to be Daddy's girl?

Michael Longley

The War Graves

The exhausted cathedral reaches nowhere near the sky
As though behind its buttresses wounded angels
Snooze in a halfway house of gargoyles, rainwater
By the mouthful, broken wings among pigeons' wings.

There will be no end to clearing up after the war
And only an imaginary harvest-home where once
The Germans drilled holes for dynamite, for fieldmice
To smuggle seeds and sow them inside these columns.

The headstones wipe out the horizon like a blizzard
And we can see no farther than the day they died,
As though all of them died together on the same day
And the war was that single momentous explosion.

Mothers and widows pruned these roses yesterday,
It seems, planted sweet william and mowed the lawn
After consultations with the dead, heads meeting
Over this year's seed catalogues and packets of seeds.

Around the shell holes not one poppy has appeared,
No symbolic flora, only the tiny whitish flowers
No one remembers the names of in time, brookweed
And fairy flax, say, lamb's lettuce and penny-cress.

In mine craters so vast they are called after cities
Violets thrive, as though strewn by each cataclysm
To sweeten the atmosphere and conceal death's smell
With a perfume that vanishes as soon as it is found.

At the Canadian front line permanent sandbags
And duckboards admit us to the underworld, and then
With the beavers we surface for long enough to hear
The huge lamentations of the wounded caribou.

Old pals in the visitors' book at Railway Hollow
Have scribbled 'The severest spot. The lads did well'
'We came to remember', and the woodpigeons too
Call from the wood and all the way from Accrington.

I don't know how Rifleman Parfitt, Corporal Vance,
Private Costello of the Duke of Wellingtons,
Driver Chapman, Topping, Atkinson, Duckworth,
Dorrell, Wood come to be written in my diary.

For as high as we can reach we touch-read the names
Of the disappeared, and shut our eyes and listen to
Finches' chitters and a blackbird's apprehensive cry
Accompanying Charles Sorley's monumental sonnet.

We describe the comet at Edward Thomas's grave
And, because he was a fisherman, that headlong
Motionless deflection looks like a fisherman's fly,
Two or three white after-feathers overlapping.

Geese on sentry duty, lambs, a clattering freight train
And a village graveyard encompass Wilfred Owen's
Allotment, and there we pick from a nettle bed
One celandine each, the flower that outwits winter.

Roddy Lumsden

Yeah Yeah Yeah

No matter what you did to her, she said,
There's times, she said, she misses you, your face
Will pucker in her dream, and times the bed's
Too big. Stray hairs will surface in a place
You used to leave your shoes. A certain phrase,
Some old song on the radio, a joke
You had to be there for, she said, some days
It really gets to her; the way you smoked
Or held a cup, or her, and how you woke
Up crying in the night sometimes, the way
She'd stroke and hush you back, and how you broke
Her still. All this she told me yesterday,
Then she rolled over, laughed, began to do
To me what she so rarely did with you.

Derek Mahon

DEATH IN BANGOR

We stand – not many of us – in a new cemetery
on a cold hillside in the north of Co. Down
staring at an open grave or out to sea,
the lough half-hidden by great drifts of rain.
Only a few months since you were snug at home
in a bungalow glow, keeping provincial time
in the chimney corner, *News-Letter* and *Woman's Own*
on your knee, wool-gathering by Plato's firelight,
a grudging flicker of flame on anthracite.
Inactive since your husband died, your chief
concern the 'appearances' that ruled your life
in a neighbourhood of bay windows and stiff
gardens shivering in the salt sea air,
the rising-sun motif on door and gate,
you knew the secret history of needlework,
bread-bin and laundry basket awash with light,
the straight-backed chairs, the madly chiming clock.
The figure in the *Republic* returns to the cave,
a Dutch interior where cloud-shadows move,
to examine the intimate spaces, chest and drawer,
the lavender in the linen, the savings book,
the kitchen table silent with nobody there.
Shall we say the patience of an angel? No,
not unless angels be thought anxious too
and God knows you had reason to be; for yours
was an anxious time of nylon and bakelite,
market-driven hysteria on every fretwork radio,
your frantic kitsch decor designed for you
by thick industrialists and twisted ministers
('Nature's a bad example to simple folk'); and yet
with your wise monkeys and euphemistic 'Dresden' figurines,
your junk chinoiserie and coy pastoral scenes,
you too were a kind of artist, a rage-for-order freak

setting against a man's aesthetic of cars and golf
your ornaments and other breakable stuff.
Visible from your window the sixth-century
abbey church of Colum and Malachi,
'light of the world' once in the monastic ages,
home of antiphonary and the radiant pages
of shining scripture; though you had your own
idea of the beautiful, not unrelated to Tolstoy
but formed in a tough city of ships and linen,
Harland & Wolff, Mackie's, Gallaher's, Lyle & Kinahan
and your own York St. Flax Spinning Co. Ltd.,
where you worked with a thousand others before the war;
of trams and shopping arcades, dance-hall and 'milk bar',
cold picnics at Whitehead and Donaghadee,
of Henry Joy McCracken and Wolfe Tone,
a glimmer of hope indefinitely postponed,
daft musicals at the Curzon and the Savoy;
later, a bombing raid glimpsed from your bedroom window,
utility clothing, US armoured divisions here,
the dwindling industries. (Where now the great
liners that raised their bows at the end of the street?
Ophidian shapes among the chandeliers,
wood-boring organisms at the swirling stairs.)
Beneath a Castilian sky, at a great mystic's rococo tomb,
I thought of the plain Protestant fatalism of home.
Remember 1690; prepare to meet thy God.
I grew up among washing-lines and grey skies,
pictures of Brookeborough on the gable-ends,
revolvers, RUC, B-Specials, law-'n'-order,
a hum of drums above the summer glens
echoing like *Götterdämmerung* over lough water
in a violent post-industrial sunset blaze
while you innocently hummed 'South of the Border',
'On a Slow Boat to China', 'Beyond the Blue Horizon'.
…Little soul, the body's guest and companion,
this is a cold epitaph from your only son,
the wish genuine if the tone ambiguous.

Oh, I can love you now that you're dead and gone
to the many mansions in your mother's house.
All artifice stripped away, we give you back to nature
but something of you, perhaps the incurable ache
of art, goes with me as I travel south
past misty drumlins, shining lanes to the shore,
above the Mournes a final helicopter,
sun-showers and rainbows all the way through Louth,
cottages buried deep in ivy and rhododendron,
ranch houses, dusty palms, blue skies of the republic...

Glyn Maxwell

MY GRANDFATHER AT THE POOL

i.m. James Maxwell 1895-1980

This photo I know best of him is him
With pals of his about to take a swim,

Forming a line with four of them, so five
All told one afternoon, about to dive:

Merseysiders, grinning and wire-thin,
Still balanced, not too late to not go in,

Or feint to but then teeter on a whim.
The only one who turned away is him,

About to live the trenches and survive,
Alone, as luck would have it, of the five.

Four gazing at us levelly, one not.
Another pal decided on this shot,

Looked down into the box and said *I say*
And only James looked up and then away.

I narrow my own eyes until they blur.
In a blue sneeze of a cornfield near Flers

In 1969, he went *Near here*

It happened and he didn't say it twice.
It's summer and the pool will be like ice.

Five pals in Liverpool about to swim.
The only one who looks away is him.

The other four look steadily across
The water and the joke they share to us.

Wholly and coldly gone, they meet our eyes
Like stars the eye is told are there and tries

To see – all pity flashes back from there,
Till I too am the unnamed unaware

And things are stacked ahead of me so vast
I sun myself in shadows that they cast:

Things I dreamt but never dreamt were there,
But are and may by now be everywhere.

When you're what turns the page or looks away.
When I'm what disappears into my day.

Roger McGough

THE WAY THINGS ARE

No, the candle is not crying, it cannot feel pain.
Even telescopes, like the rest of us, grow bored.
Bubblegum will not make the hair soft and shiny.
The duller the imagination, the faster the car –
I am your father and this is the way things are

When the sky is looking the other way,
do not enter the forest. No, the wind
is not caused by the rushing of clouds.
An excuse is as good a reason as any.
A lighthouse, launched, will not go far –
I am your father and this is the way things are

No, old people do not walk slowly
because they have plenty of time.
Gardening books when buried will not flower.
Though lightly worn, a crown may leave a scar –
I am your father and this is the way things are

No, the red woolly hat has not been
put on the railing to keep it warm.
When one glove is missing, both are lost.
Today's craft fair is tomorrow's car boot sale.
The guitarist gently weeps, not the guitar –
I am your father and this is the way things are

Pebbles work best without batteries.
The deckchair will fail as a unit of currency.
Even though your shadow is shortening
it does not mean you are growing smaller.
Moonbeams sadly, will not survive in a jar –
I am your father and this is the way things are

For centuries the bullet remained quietly confident
that the gun would be invented.
A drowning Dadaist will not appreciate
the concrete lifebelt.
No guarantee my last goodbye is au revoir –
I am your father and this is the way things are

Do not become a prison-officer unless you know
what you're letting someone else in for.
The thrill of being a shower curtain will soon pall.
No trusting hand awaits the falling star –
I am your father, and I am sorry,
but this is the way things are.

Jamie McKendrick

Home Thoughts

The airmail from India, a weatherbeaten blue,
with wax marks from the candle you had used
to write by reached me. You write that reach
is what travellers there do rather than arrive
being more respectful to the gods of place.
For years your letters from around the world
have kept on reaching me wherever
I'm hunched beside an atlas and a lamp.
When you last saw me I was living in a room
across the road from but a floor below
the room we used to share ten years ago.
Only kindness stopped you saying
it took me quite some time to cross that road;
and looking from my window I expect to see
myself looking out to where in ten years time
I'll be looking back again to see... the last things
you mention are the Parsee towers of silence
where the dead are left for vultures to attend.
I warm to that. It sort of brings things home.

Angela McSeveney

KIRSTY

The radio reports the disappearance
of a seven year-old wearing a blue
quilted jacket and brown lacing shoes.

My stomach clenches
as it did thirteen years before
on an empty building site.

The cement bag spread beneath me
stuck to my back.

Robert Minhinnick

TWENTY-FIVE LAMENTS FOR IRAQ

The muzzein voices break the night
Telling us of what we are composed:
Coffee grits; a transparency of sugar;
The ghost of the cardomom in the cup's mosque.

These soldiers will not marry.
They are wed already
To the daughters of uranium.

Sherazade sits
In heat and dust
Watching her bucket fill.
This is the first story.

Before hunger
        Thirst.
Before prayer
        Thirst.
Before money
        Thirst.
Before thirst.
        Water.

Boys of Watts and Jones County
Build cookfires on the ramparts of Ur.
But the desert birds are silent
And all the wolves of the province
Fled to the north.

While we are filming the sick child
The sick child behind us
Dies. And as we turn our camera
The family group smartens itself

As if grieving might offend.

Red and gold
The baldaquins
Beneath the Baghdad moon,
Beneath the Pepsi globe.

Since the first Caliph
There has been the *suq* –
These lemons, this fish:
And hunched over the stone
The women in their black –
Four dusty aubergines.

My daughter, he says,
Stroking the Sony DV Cam,
Its batteries hot, the tally light red.
My daughter.

But his daughter, 12, keeps to her cot,
Woo woo wooing like the hoopoe
Over the British cemetery.

What are children here
But olivestones under our shoes?
Reach instead for the date
Before its brilliance tarnishes.

Back and forth
Back and forth
The Euphrates kingfisher,
The ferryman's rope.

The ice seller waits
Beneath his thatch of palm,
His money running in the gutter's tilth.

Over the searchlights
And machine gun nests on Rashid Street
The bats explode like tracer fire.

Yellow as dates these lizards
Bask on the basilica.
Our cameraman removes his shoes,
Squats down to pray.

Radiant,
With the throat of a shark,
The angel who came to the hundreds
Sheltered in Amariya.

In the hotel carpark
One hundred and fifty brides and grooms
Await the photographer.
All night I lie awake
Listening to their cries.

This first dollar peeled off the wad
Buys a stack of dinars higher than my heart.

A heron in white
And a woman in black
Knee deep together
In the green Tigris.

Her two pomegranates lie beside the bed
But they have carried the child away.

She alights from the bus
In a cloud of black,
The moon and stars upon her skirt,
And painted across her breast
The Eye that Sees All Things.

The vermilion on his toenails
        Is almost worn away,
This child of the bazaar
Who rolls my banknote to a tube
And scans through its telescope
The ruins of Babylon.

Four billion years
Until the uranium
That was spilled at Ur
Unmakes itself.
Easier to wait for the sun to die.

In the Ministry of Information
Computers are down, the offices dark;
But with me in the corridor
A secret police of cockroaches.

Moths, I say.
No. Look again, she suggests.
Fused to the ceiling are the black hands
Of the children of Amariya.

        Sometimes
The certainties return:
These cushions, a pipe,
And the sweet Basran tea
Stewed with limes.

Andrew Motion

Fresh Water
In Memory of Ruth Haddon

1

This is a long time ago. I am visiting my brother, who is living
near Cirencester, and he says let's go and see the source of the
                                        Thames.
It's winter. We leave early, before the sun has taken frost off the
                                        fields,

and park in a lane. There's a painful hawthorn hedge with a
                                        stile.
When we jump down, our boots gibber on the hard ground.
Then we're striding, kicking ice-dust off the grass to look
                                confident –

because really we're not sure if we're allowed to be here.
In fact we're not even sure that this is the right place.
A friend of a friend has told us; it's all as vague as that.

In the centre of the field we find more hawthorn, a single
                                        bush,
and water oozing out of a hole in the ground. I tell my brother
I've read about a statue that stands here, or rather lounges
                                        here –

a naked, shaggy-haired god tilting an urn with one massive
                                        hand.
Where is he? There's only the empty field glittering,
and a few dowager cows picking among the dock-clumps.

Where is Father Thames? My brother thinks he has been
vandalised
and dragged off by the fans of other rivers – they smashed the
old man's urn,
and sprayed his bare chest and legs with the names of rivals:

Trent, Severn, Nene, Humber. There's nothing else to do,
so I paddle through the shallow water surrounding the spring,
treading carefully to keep things in focus,

and stoop over the source as though I find it fascinating.
It is fascinating. A red-brown soft-lipped cleft
with bright green glass right up to the edge,

and the water twisting out like a rope of glass.
It pulses and shivers as it comes, then steadies
into the pool, then roughens again as it drains into the valley.

My brother and I are not twenty yet. We don't know who we
are,
Or who we want to be. We stare at the spring, at each other,
and back at the spring again, saying nothing.

A pheasant is making its blatant *kok-kok*
from the wood running along the valley floor.
I stamp both feet and disappear in a cloud.

2

One March there's suddenly a day as warm as May, and my
friend
uncovers the punt he has bought as a wreck and restored,
cleans her, slides her into the Thames near Lechlade, and sets off

upriver. Will I go with him? No, I can't.
But I'll meet him on the water meadows at the edge of town.
I turn out of the market square, past the church, and down
                                        the yew-tree walk.

Shelley visited here once – it's called Shelley's Walk –
but he was out of his element. Here everything is earth
and water, not fire and air. The ground is sleepy-haired

after winter, red berries and rain matted into it.
Where the yew-tree walk ends I go blind in the sun for a
                                        moment,
then it's all right. There's the river beyond the boggy meadows,

hidden by reed-forests sprouting along its banks. They're
                                        dead,
the reeds – a shambles of broken, broad, pale-brown leaves
and snapped bullrush heads. And there's my friend making

his slow curve towards me. The hills rise behind him
in a gradual wave, so that he seems at the centre of an enormous
amphitheatre. He is an emblem of something;

somebody acting something. The punt pole shoots up
wagging its beard of light, falls, and as he moves ahead
he leans forward, red-faced and concentrating.

He's expert but it's slow work. As I get closer I can hear
water pattering against the prow of the punt,
see him twisting the pole as he plucks it out of the gluey
                                        river-bed.

I call to him and he stands straight, giving a wobbly wave.
We burst into laughter. He looks like a madman, floating
                                        slowly
backwards now that he has stopped poling. I must look

like a madman too, mud-spattered and heavy-footed on the
                                                   bank,
wondering how I'm going to get on board without falling in.
As I push open the curtain of leaves to find a way,

I see the water for the first time, solid-seeming and mercury-
                                            coloured.
Not like a familiar thing at all. Not looking
as though it could take us anywhere we wanted to go.

3

I've lived here for a while, and up to now the river has been
for pleasure. This evening people in diving suits have taken it
                                                   over.
Everyone else has been shooshed away into Christchurch
                                        Meadow

or onto Folly Bridge like me. No one's complaining. The
                                        summer evening
expands lazily, big purple and gold clouds building over the
                                        Cumnor hills.
I have often stood here before. Away to the left you can see
                                        Oxford

throwing its spires into the air, full of the conceited joy of
                                        being itself.
Straight ahead the river runs calmly between boat-houses
before losing patience again, pulling a reed-shawl round its ears,

snapping off willows and holding their scarified heads
                                        underwater.
Now there's a small rowing boat, a kind of coracle below me,
and two policemen with their jackets off. The men shield their
                                        eyes,

peering, and almost rock overboard, they're so surprised,
when bubbles erupt beside them and a diver bobs up –
just his head, streaming in its black wet-suit. There are shouts –

See anything? – but the diver shrugs, and twirls his murky
                                        torchlight
with an invisible hand. Everyone on the bridge stops talking.
We think we are about to be shown the story of the river-bed –

its shopping trolleys and broken boat-parts, its lolling bottles,
its plastic, its dropped keys, its blubbery and bloated corpse.
But nothing happens. The diver taps his mask and disappears,

his fart-trail surging raucously for a moment, then subsiding.
The crowd in Christchurch Meadow starts to break up.
On Folly Bridge people begin talking again, and as someone
                                        steps

off the pavement onto the road, a passing grocery van –
irritated by the press of people, and impatient with whatever
brought them together – gives a long wild *paarp* as it revs
                                        away.

    4

Now the children are old enough to see what there is to see
we take them to Tower Bridge and explain how the road lifts up,
how traitors arrived at Traitor's Gate, how this was a brewery

and that was a warehouse, how the river starts many miles
                                        inland
and changes and grows, changes and grows, until it arrives here,
London, where we live, then winds past Canary Wharf

(which they've done in school) and out to sea.
Afterwards we lean on the railings outside a café. It's autumn.
The water is speckled with leaves, and a complicated tangle of
                                                                    junk

bumps against the embankment wall: a hank of bright grass,
a rotten bullrush stem, a fragment of dark polished wood.
One of the children asks if people drown in the river, and I
                                                                    think

of Ruth, who was on the *Marchioness*. After her death, I met
someone who had survived. He had been in the lavatory when
                                                                    the dredger hit,
and fumbled his way out along a flooded corridor, his shoes

and clothes miraculously slipping off him, so that when he at
                                                                    last
burst into the air he felt that he was a baby again
and knew nothing, was unable to help himself, aghast.

I touch my wife's arm and the children gather round us.
We are the picture of a family on an outing. I love it. I love the
                                                                    river
and the perky tour-boats with their banal chat. I love the snub
                                                                    barges.

I love the whole dazzling cross-hatchery of traffic and currents,
shadows and sun, standing still and moving forward.
The tangle of junk bumps the wall below me again and I look
                                                                    down.

There is Ruth swimming back upstream, her red velvet party
                                                                    dress
flickering round her heels as she twists through the locks
and dreams round the slow curves, slithering on for miles

until she has passed the ponderous diver at Folly Bridge
and the reed-forests at Lechlade, accelerating beneath bridges
                                    and willow branches,
slinking easily among the plastic wrecks and weedy trolleys,

speeding and shrinking and silvering until finally she is sliding
                                    uphill
over bright green grass and into the small wet mouth of the
                                    earth,
where she vanishes.

Paul Muldoon

WIRE

As I roved out this morning at daybreak
I took a short cut
through the pine forest, following the high-tension wires
past the timber line
till I stumbled upon a makeshift hide or shooting-box
from which a command-wire seemed to run

intermittently along the ski-run
or fire-break.
I glanced into the hideout. A school lunch-box.
A pear so recently cut
I thought of Ceylon. A can of Valvoline.
Crocodile clips. Sri Lanka, I mean. A hank of wire

that might come in handy if ever I'd want to hot-wire
a motor and make a run
for the border. From just beyond my line
of vision I glimpsed something, or someone, break
cover for an instant. A shaved head, maybe, or a crewcut.
Jumping up like a jack-in-the-box

before ducking back down. Then a distant raking through the
    gear-box
of a truck suddenly gone haywire
on this hillside of hillsides in Connecticut
brought back some truck on a bomb run,
brought back so much with which I'd hoped to break –
the hard-line

yet again refusing to toe the line,
the bullet and the ballot box,
the joy-ride, the jail-break,
Janet endlessly singing 'The Men behind the Wire',

the endless re-run
of Smithfield, La Mon, Enniskillen, of bodies cut
to ribbons as I heard the truck engine cut
and, you might have read as much between the lines,
ducked down here myself behind the hide. As if I myself were on
    the run.
The truck driver handing a box-
cutter, I'm sure, to the bald guy. A pair of real live wires.
I've listened to them all day now, between making a break

for it and their talk of the long run, the short term, of boxing
    clever,
fish or cut bait, make or break,
the end of the line, right down to the wire.

Les Murray

THE SHIELD-SCALES OF HERALDRY

Surmounting my government's high evasions
stands a barbecue of crosses and birds
tended by a kangaroo and emu
but in our courts, above the judge,
a lion and a unicorn still keep
their smaller offspring, plus a harp,
in an open prison looped with mottoes.

Coats of arms, plaster Rorschach blots,
crowned stone moths, they encrust Europe.
As God was dismissed from churches
they fluttered in and cling to the walls,
abstract comic-pages held by scrolled beasts,
or wear on the flagstones underfoot.
They pertain to an earlier Antichrist,

the one before police. Mafiose citadels
made them, states of one attended family
islanded in furrows. The oldest
are the simplest. A cross, some coins,
a stripe, a roof tree, a spur rowel,
bowstaves, a hollow-gutted lion,
and all in lucid target colours.

The rhyming of name with name,
marriages quarter and cube them
till they are sacred campaign maps
or anatomy inside dissected mantling,
glyphs minutely clear through their one
rule, that colour must abut either
gold or silver, the non-weapon metals.

The New World doesn't blazon well –
the new world ran away from blazonry
or was sent away in chains by it –
but exceptions shine: the spread eagle
with the fireworks display on its belly
and in the thinks-balloon above its head.
And when as a half-autistic

kid in scrub paddocks vert and or
I grooved on the cloisons of pedigree
it was a vivid writing of system
that hypnotised me, beyond the obvious
euphemism of force. It was eight hundred
years of cubist art and Europe's dreamings:
the Cup, the Rose, the Ship, the Antlers.

High courage, bestial snobbery,
neither now merits ungrace from us.
They could no longer hang me,
throttling, for a rabbit sejant.
Like everyone, I would now be lord
or lady myself, and pardon me
or myself loose the coronet-necked hounds.

Stephanie Norgate

THE WHEEDLING MAN

Just because he spoke in a wheedling sort of way,
just because he looked ashamed and afraid,
just because he whined and crouched,
just because he was so aware of his lost life,
fingering the old bus-pass in his pocket,
the photograph of his wife, just because
he drew his jacket round him against the cold
even though it was a warm blue day,
just because he puckered his face and looked like he might cry,
or suddenly piss on the venerable paving stones,
just because he wouldn't let up, was desperate
and sad, I didn't give him anything.
And now it's no consolation
to the hungry wheedling man, that he's stayed in my head
and won't go away, that I can replay every word of what he said,
how he looked; that I'm still walking down the lovely old alleyway
with its famous trace of an open sewer,
swishing my feet in gold-fingered horsechestnut leaves,
thinking of this man I meet everyday at four for sex,
(but not so crudely as that, in a kind of haze)
when he gets up from under the wall and approaches me,
his voice whining in my ear, his tweedy jacket
brushing my shoulder,
please love love please love spare me some change
dancing in front of me, stopping me getting on.
But two hours earlier, a man
with matted hair and Rasputin eyes
said to me firmly, 'I need two pounds. Give it me.'
And I gave instantly.

Sean O'Brien

When I walk by your house, I spit.
That's not true. I *intend* to.
When you're at breakfast with the *Daily Mail*
Remember me. I'm here about this time,
Disabled by restraint and staring.
But I do not send the bag of excrement,
Decapitate your dog at night,
Or press you to a glass of Paraquat,
Or hang you by your bollocks from a tree,
Still less conceal the small home-made device
Which blows your head off, do I, prat?
I think you'll have to grant me that,
Because I haven't. But I might.
If I were you, I'd be afraid of me.

Bernard O'Donoghue

And now I long to be a poet/With something good to say.
(i.m. Denis O'Connor, 1918-97)

Just as I'm happier walking in the dark
Of night and feel more safe in planes
Than on the ground, I'm less at ease
Among the living than the dead.
For years I've specialized in writing
Letters to the bereaved, a brief
From a licensed afterlife, consoling
Children, widowers and widows.

But who am I to write to you about you,
Denis, who made your own way? I'd like
To honour your unrivalled singing,
Your melojeon, and your wit-barbs;
Your merriment among the dancers,
And your vamped mouth-organ. Who do I remind
How you could run up the twenty rungs
Of a ladder standing in the middle
Of the yard, our stilted boy?

You had the excitement of the hare,
And a like form, away from the everyday.
You had the fox's glamour, the perfectly
Made out-of-the-ordinariness
Of that thrush's nest, sealed with spit,
You showed us above the arum lilies.
We admired, but didn't understand
That you were Hermes, bearing messages
From the past, and must return, like summer
Out over the top of the fairy-thimbles.

Who dug your grave, Denis,
Since you dug everyone's?
Who carried your coffin?
There's no one in the parish
Who would not push to the front
Of the crowd to bear you.
Are we now at liberty to call you
Dansel, the venerated, unaccounted-for
Nickname of your family,
That no-one spoke in your presence –
Out of some sentiment: tact? or fear?
Love maybe. In the silence
After your death, may we speak it now?

In the grave, shall all be renewed?
Your celebrity? Will this letter do?
No: by way of postscript I remind us all
Of a late-December night when you were old
And sick and looking for a drive
To help you get your messages up home.
It wasn't easy to make out what
You were mumbling, with the drink.
"Christmas is the worst time of all
For the person living on their own."

Sharon Olds

Mrs Krikorian

She saved me. When I arrived in sixth grade
a known criminal, the new teacher
asked me to stay after school the first day, she said
I've heard about you. She was a tall woman,
with a deep crevice between her breasts,
and a large, calm nose. She said,
This is a special library pass.
As soon as you finish your hour's work –
that hour's work that took ten minutes
and then the devil glanced into the room
and found me empty, a house standing open –
you can go to the library. Every hour
I'd zip through the work, and slip out of
my seat as if out of God's side and sail
down to the library, down through the empty
powerful halls, flash my pass
and stroll over to the dictionary
to look up the most interesting word
I knew, *spank*, dipping two fingers
into the jar of library paste to
suck that tart mucilage as I
came to the page with the cocker spaniel's
silks curling up like the fine steam of the body.
After *spank*, and *breast*, I'd move on
to *Abe Lincoln* and *Helen Keller*,
safe in their goodness till the bell, thanks
to Mrs Krikorian, amiable giantess
with the kind eyes. When she asked me to write
a play, and direct it, and it was a flop,
and I hid in the coat closet, she bought me a candy-cane
as you lay a peppermint on the tongue, and the worm
will come up out of the bowel to get it.
And so I was emptied of Lucifer

and filled with school glue and eros and
Amelia Earhart, saved by Mrs Krikorian.
And who had saved Mrs Krikorian?
When the Turks came across Armenia,
who slid her into the belly of a quilt, who
locked her in a chest, who mailed her to America?
And *that* one, who saved *her*, and *that* one –
who saved *her*, to save the one
who saved Mrs Krikorian, who was
standing there on the sill of sixth grade, a
wide-hipped angel, smoky hair
standing up lightly all around her head?
I end up owing my soul to so many,
to the Armenian nation, one more soul someone
jammed behind a stove, drove
deep into a crack in a wall,
shoved under a bed. I would wake
up, in the morning, under my bed – not
knowing how I had got there – and lie
in the dusk, the dustballs beside my face
round and ashen, shining slightly
with the eerie comfort of what is neither good nor evil.

Alice Oswald

My Neighbour, Mrs Kersey

That noise, Mrs Kersey—were you listening?
A tin roof warping and booming . . .

Our sitting rooms connect like shears
into the screw-pin of our fires.

We share a bird's nest in a common chimney.
If I'm right, you breathe, Mrs Kersey,

close as a dream-self on the other side.
This wall, if you just rubbed an eyelid,

is a bricked-up looking glass.
And wind across that roof's a loss

of difference to whatever's moving
privately through our heads this evening.

Like the clicking of my jaw,
the tic-tac of your solitaire.

Ruth Padel

CASCAVEL

We want to see how gems get made in Rio.
How jewel-hunters of Brazil are feather-probing,
As we speak, the red-earth mines
And those shadow-dancing caves and mountain streams,
    Where mythic venom-pushers like the *fer de lance*
Are ambushing nine (at least) species of gold and emerald frog
From under fallen logs. How rotating knife-wheels,
Dusted with diamond, release the voodoo-shine

Of morganite from ruddy gobs of neo-slingshot.
How you tell a good one by comparing it to master stones
    Picked out by crystallographers. We want
Jewel-surgeons, droves of them, in action,
Making the perfect cut. 'Marquise', 'Brilliante', 'Classic Drop'.

Well – fine. We get the lot. An eyeful of Brazilian tourmaline
In pink, blue, yellow, green. Citrine, to see off nightmares.
Amethyst, keeping you sober whatever the alcohol
Consumed. Emeralds with veins like fern,
    The beaten silk and cyanide of peridot
In its hibernated state. The burn
Of rubies, ghost-pale chrysoprase. And diamonds everywhere
Like dandruff. But then we get fed through to Sales –

To Rosa Klebb, the torturer from early-mid James Bond,
Plus rows of senior citizens – couples who just rolled up, like us,
    To take a look, and found themselves in second honeymoon
                                                              pose
Facing banks of Tiger Eye and Sherry Beryl, that set you back
Three thousand. All the sparklers, stones men hack

From mountains, rank, grind, set in gold
And buy for women to wear. 'What do you want to see?'

What do you think? An amber wedding wreath? A kingsize bed
With platinum sheets? That matching pair
    Of sapphire watches trimmed
With custard-gold gold leaf?
We're fine, thanks, as we are.
Years, now, we've worn rings

We gave each other, since you turned up with
(You said) a leopardskin bra, and smuggled an opal
    On my finger, here, instead. 'You're interested
In opals?' She shimmies us three trays. 'An opal is
Like pumice – soft. The flicks of fire,

These points of pink, blue, yellow, green,
Are billions – look – of water drops.
The more there are, more colour in the stone,
The more expensive.' Please. What *are* we doing here
    When we could be in the forest, or a bar?
Getting into opal hierarchies, you spot the really rare
One. 'Is she open Saturday?' Jesus. You'll be asking next
For credit facilities or Euro-checks. I slither us out

To the jungle's tapestries, wagon wheels of umbrella-fern
Glowing and glancing with rain
    Plus a drum-roll blues from five
(At least) species of frog. Sheer night falls, instantly, Fritz,
Whom we blindly trust (or do we?), goes ahead across the
                                                    stream

And up the mountain path with two big sticks, poking
Every pile of leaves, every loose (but pitch-black) rock.
My canvas-and-Velcro sandals (wet, no socks) follow the steps
Of your Nike trainers. Hand in hand, Indian file,
    Eros and Psyche under the Telephone Tree
(Whose lianas are ready to brain us), my freezing fingers up
Your sleeve, we sing to warn the snakes we're here.
'Rose of Tralee'. 'Moon River'. Hours later, soaking, we reach

A blue-tiled hut. The guard mixes sugarcane-husk
Martinis. Doubles. We admire his wall-art –
  Posters of eight local species of *cascavel*
(A.k.a. rattlesnake), each
Of whose bite leaves seven hours to live. Back home in the
                                                    hotel,

Your PowerBook glistering with ants, the desk-lamp throws
A floating amber fan from your head around the wall,
And Rio roars outside. Alone,
Dry, safe (amazingly), we're both at work
  Above loonily perfect Copacabana Beach
Where little boys, lime green and glitter-rose,
Play manic soccer in soft sapphire dusk
To an audience of rearing, floodlit, diamond surf.

Don Paterson

Nil Nil

Just as any truly accurate representation of a particular geography can only exist on a scale of 1:1 (imagine the vast, rustling map of Burgundy, say, settling over it like a freshly-starched sheet!) so it is with all our abandoned histories, those ignoble lines of succession that end in neither triumph nor disaster, but merely plunge on into deeper and deeper obscurity; only in the infinite ghost-libraries of the imagination – their only possible analogue – can their ends be pursued, the dull and terrible facts finally authenticated.

Francois Aussemain, Pensées

From the top, then, the zenith, the silent footage:
McGrandle, majestic in ankle-length shorts,
his golden hair shorn to an open book, sprinting
the length of the park for the long hoick forward,
his balletic toe-poke nearly bursting the roof
of the net; a shaky pan to the Erskine St End
where a plague of grey bonnets falls out of the clouds.
But ours is a game of two halves, and this game
the semi they went on to lose; from here
it's all down, from the First to the foot of the Second,
McGrandle, Visocchi and Spankie detaching
like bubbles to speed the descent into pitch-sharing,
pay-cuts, pawned silver, the Highland Division,
the absolute sitters ballooned over open goals,
the dismal nutmegs, the scores so obscene
no respectable journal will print them; though one day
Farquhar's spectacular bicycle-kick
will earn him a name-check in Monday's obituaries.
Besides the one setback – the spell of giant-killing
in the Cup (Lochee Violet, then Aberdeen Bon Accord,
the deadlock with Lochee Harp finally broken
by Farquhar's own-goal in the replay)

nothing inhibits the fifty-year slide
into Sunday League, big tartan flasks,
open hatchbacks parked squint behind goal-nets,
the half-time satsuma, the dog on the pitch,
then the Boy's Club, sponsored by Skelly Assurance,
then Skelly Dry Cleaners, then nobody;
stud-harrowed pitches with one-in-five inclines,
grim fathers and perverts with Old English Sheepdogs
lining the touch, moaning softly.
Now the unrefereed thirty-a-sides,
terrified fat boys with callipers minding
four jackets on infinite, notional fields;
ten years of dwindling, half-hearted kickabouts
leaves two little boys – Alastair Watt,
who answers to 'Forty', and wee Horace Madden,
so smelly the air seems to quiver above him –
playing desperate two-touch with a bald tennis ball
in the hour before lighting-up time.
Alastair cheats, and goes off with the ball
leaving wee Horace to hack up a stone
and dribble it home in the rain;
past the stopped swings, the dead shanty-town
of allotments, the black shell of Skelly Dry Cleaners
and into his cul-de-sac, where, accidentally,
he neatly back-heels it straight into the gutter
then tries to swank off like he meant it.

Unknown to him, it is all that remains
of a lone fighter-pilot, who, returning at dawn
to find Leuchars was not where he'd left it,
took time out to watch the Sidlaws unsheathed
from their great black tarpaulin, the haar burn off Tayport
and Venus melt into Carnoustie, igniting
the shoreline; no wind, not a cloud in the sky
and no one around to admire the discretion
of his unscheduled exit: the engine plopped out
and would not re-engage, sending him silently

twirling away like an ash-key,
his attempt to bail out only partly successful,
yesterday having been April the 1st –
the ripcord unleashing a flurry of socks
like a sackful of doves rendered up to the heavens
in private irenicon. He caught up with the plane
on the ground, just at the instant the tank blew
and made nothing of him, save for his fillings,
his tackets, his lucky half-crown and his gallstone,
now anchored between the steel bars of a stank
that looks to be biting the bullet on this one.

In short, this is where you get off, reader;
I'll continue alone, on foot, in the failing light
following the trail as it steadily fades
into road-repairs, birdsong, the weather, nirvana,
the plot thinning down to a point so refined
not even the angels could dance on it. Goodbye.

Evangeline Paterson

LUCIFER AT THE FAIR

Blowing my last bob
on the Jungle Ride, I saw him.
Tawny and lithe as a hunting
cat, he balanced and swayed
on the racketing heave of the boards.
I whirled like an atom around him

to thunderous music. He took
my shilling, gazing aloof,
while I, thin as a lizard,
with skinned knees, went bucketing
past, uncoveted prize in my
striped school dress. If he'd spoken
a word to me, I'd have died.

For hours I lay, seeing,
printed on night, him
glow like a dark angel
at the heart of his whirring planet.

Brian Patten

THE ARMADA

Long long ago
when everything I was told was believable
and the little I knew was less limited than now,
I stretched belly down on the grass beside a pond
and to the far bank launched a child's armada.
A broken fortress of twigs,
the paper-tissue sails of galleons,
the waterlogged branches of submarines –
all came to ruin and were on flame
in that dusk-red pond.
And you, mother, stood behind me,
impatient to be going,
old at twenty-three, alone,
thin overcoat flapping.
How closely the past shadows us.
In a hospital a mile or so from that pond
I kneel beside your bed and, closing my eyes,
reach out across forty years to touch once more
that pond's cool surface,
and it is your cool skin I'm touching;
for as on a pond a child's paper boat
was blown out of reach
by the smallest gust of wind,
so too have you been blown out of reach
by the smallest whisper of death,
and a childhood memory is sharpened,
and the heart burns as that armada burnt,
long, long ago.

Tom Paulin

Drumcree Four

The preacher
you know that costive overreacher
the mate of biblebashing lechers
says the Twelfth will be the settling
time then reaches
for his blackthorn
and marches to the barricade
– no more
flicks this time of the Orange Card
– they're in a tribal huff
it is a standoff

I listen to the radio
I read the papers
but how this caper
will end no one knows
only the word *settle*
its clanky its metallic
even archaic sound
hits the ear
like listening to a battered kettle
or a tin can
being kicked across a patch
of rocky ground
or concrete walkway
– should we cut an eyepatch
for the pirate preacher
then snap his stick?
he claims this patch of ground's
his tribe's alone
and through a megaphone
he gulders with a deep thick
ululating wheezing sound

that strains like Ulster
in a bulging holster
that bible uniform
pressed by what his father stuck
to – now watch the British state
as with fairness and no hate
it grasps the nettle
and says – walk? no way

M R Peacocke

GOOSE HYMN

We lub us ogre
It like we   two legi
Two blue eye
It dict us born

It warm us   dict us lib
It look us lub   feed us
goin out   comin in
Mind it mangly boot

It go unwingly
Lub it corni corni cop ya
Mind it strangly finger
it strongly anger

It frighten we
It mighty mighty alway
It might alway
might dict us die

Pauline Plummer

UNCLES AND AUNTIES

I was afraid of uncles,
with laughs like football crowds,
wearing bark coloured clothes,
taking up more space than allowed.

They smelt of cities and work.
Shirts could not contain
the bristles sprouting through collars
and cuffs, the fingers nicotine stained.

A man exposed himself
to me when I was just a kid.
Impossible to tell anyone of his revolting
pinkness, what his flapping trousers hid.

No wonder I preferred aunties –
in their flowery dresses, scrub rough hands,
faces dusted with icing sugar,
permanently permed; lips, strawberry jammed.

Peter Porter

It's August and hay-fever weather,
We've left the house in Summer's tether–
While you girls scamper hell-for-leather
    And climb the wall
Our adult hopes are all on whether
    We'll find the Earl.

The youthful Earl of Rochester
In this small parish church interred
Proclaims the triumph of the word,
    A true contrition,
For penitence is gravely heard
    In a patrician.

A bully, fiend and alcoholic,
A brilliant Hobbesean melancholic,
A frightened sinner, parabolic,
    Yet first and foremost
A mind which rendered apostolic
    Sad Reason's ghost.

What would we find if we, instead
Of looking pious, raised the lid
Of where he lies encased in lead–
    Memento mori?
I doubt it–when the flesh has fled
    All's nugatory.

His soul which bigotry would save
Is shrunk to copper in the nave,
A mere inscription. Thus the grave
    Keeps all in sight
And wife and son may only have

A year's respite.

But bouncing through the door, you girls
Pounce on the verger with skirls
Of laughter, sudden whirls and curls,
        Take up his broom,
Then, like George Herbert, for the Earl's
        Sake sweep the room.

When Martha and Amelia raise
A little dust to rightly praise
The magnitude of other days,
        They're only playing–
It's Grandad's pompous paraphrase
        Which is dismaying.

Life works the other way around:
It's what George Herbert saw which wound
His metaphor into his sound–
        A parish priest,
He'd keep his ear to the ground
        This much at least.

So give the verger back his broom
And let the Earl sleep out his doom,
I must return to London soon
        And you to Rome–
Though you're not Catholic, you assume
        There God's at home.

Is Oxfordshire more savoury
Than the ill-swept Trastevere?
Is Rome all foreign knavery?
        Our cows are mad,
Our people sunk in slavery,
        Our climate bad.

But still we speak a language which
The whole world seems to have an itch
To learn, and this may make you rich–
    England supporters–
And since you don't stray on the pitch,
    Dutiful daughters.

Sheenagh Pugh

ENVYING OWEN BEATTIE

To have stood on the Arctic island
by the graves where Franklin's men
buried their shipmates: good enough.

To hack through the permafrost
to the coffin, its loving plaque
cut from a tin can: better.

And freeing the lid, seeing
the young sailor cocooned in ice,
asleep in his glass case.

Then melting it so gently, inch
by inch, a hundred years
and more falling away, all the distance

of death a soft hiss of steam
on the air, till at last they cupped
two feet, bare and perfect,

in their hands, and choked up,
because it was any feet
poking out of the bedclothes.

And when the calm, pinched
twenty-year-old face
came free, and he lay there,

five foot four of authentic
Victorian adventurer, tuberculous,
malnourished, John Torrington

the stoker, who came so far
in the cold, and someone whispered,
It's like he's unconscious.

Then Beattie stooped, lifted him
out of bed, the six stone
limp in his arms, and the head lolled

and rested on his shoulder,
and he felt the rush
that reckless trust sends

through parents and lovers. To have him
like that, the frail, diseased
little time-traveller,

to feel the lashes prickle
your cheek, to be that close
to the parted lips.

You would know all the fairy-tales
spoke true; how could you not try
to wake him with a kiss?

Craig Raine

FROM A LA RECHERCHE DU TEMPS PERDU

So I turn to a dead language again:
ineo, I go into, enter, begin.

Doleo, I am in pain, I grieve.
And everyone thinks I am being brave.

Ignis, ignis, masculine, fire:
at St Pancras Crematorium, I stare,

light-headed with caffeine,
at the light-oak coffin,

wondering what I feel, where I stand.
Vulnus, vulneris, neuter, a wound.

I watch the coffin vanish
to Mozart on tape, its varnish

about to come up in blisters
and burst into a boa

of full-length, rustling fire,
just as we reach the Dies Irae.

Sinews shrink from the flames.
Sinews shrink in the flames.

I sentimentalise
and then revise.

Iter, itineris, neuter, a journey.
Without end. Where the road is empty.

Sine plus ablative, without.
The words are in my mouth

but I can't teach myself
the simple, difficult lesson of grief.

Too terrible to learn. Too hard
to have the words by heart.

I can't accept you're dead.
You're still here, in my head:

irritating, prickly, unsalved,
unsolved, unlovable, loved.

That bubble at the corner of your mouth.
Which seems somehow to mean so much.

Peter Reading

Man, who seldom lives a hundred years,
worries himself enough for a thousand.

Small-talk will charm a host;
straight-talk provokes dislike.

Better to die ten years early
than spend those extra years in penury.

I do not laugh at this old fart,
for I shall assuredly be thus.

Old and yellow men,
and pearls when they are yellow, are
equally worthless.

Each birthday one knows
next year will be worse.

Though we so vividly dream
of our boyhood games, our cruel mirrors
reflect snow-haired old codgers.

Deryn Rees-Jones

Lovesong to Captain James T Kirk

Captain. I never thought we'd come to this,
but things being what they are, being adults,
stardate '94 it's best to make the best of it
and laugh. What's done is done. Perhaps
I'll start to call you Jim or Jamie, James...

No one was more shocked than me when I arrived
(*the lady doth protest*) to find
my bruised and rainy planet disappeared
and me, materialised and reconstructed
on board the Starship Enterprise, all 60s
with my lacquered bee-hive and my thigh-high
skirt in blue, my Doctor Marten's and my jeans
replaced by skin-tight boots
and scratchy blue-black nylons rippling-
up my less-than-perfect calves. Sulu
looked worried. Spock cocked up one eyebrow
enigmatically, branding my existence
perfectly illogical. How nice, I thought. His ears.
Uhura smiled of course, and fiddled
with her hair. *O James*. Truth is
I loved you even as a child...

O slick-black-panted wanderer holding
your belly in, your phaser gun
on stun, and eyes like Conference pears! You're not my type
but I undress you, and we fuck
and I forgive your pancake make-up and mascara,
the darker shadows painted round your eyes.
The lava-lamp goes up and down. We're
a strange unison. Politically
Mismatched. Our mutual friend
The Doc takes notes. *Go easy Bones!*

Scotty is beaming and shouts *Energise*,
and all of a sudden you remind me
Of my dad, my brother and my mum,
my body rising like a shadow from the past
on top of you. As I press your arms behind your head
I drape my breasts so that you
brush my nipples gently with your lips almost
involuntarily as we boldly go. Come slowly, Captain,
and we do, with both our pairs of eyes tight closed.

Maurice Riordan

LAST CALL

Home late, his house asleep, a man goes to the phone,
and from habit, expecting nothing, touches the Recall.
But this time he tenses to hear the electronic scramble,
the pause before the lottery digits fall into place.
At the other end, sure enough, he hears a male voice,
no one he recognizes, repeating *Hello, hello?*
He can hear background piano, Chopin or John Field,
establishing a room, smoke-filled, larger than his,
where wine in a discarded glass is losing its chill,
while the voice continues, good-humoured, persuasive:
Come on, say something. He tries to picture a face, a hand,
to fit the voice, still in his ear, still going on, *Last chance...*
He hangs up, his own hand shaking with intimacy.

Robin Robertson

The Flaying of Marsyas
nec quicquam nisi vulnus erat (Ovid, *Metamorphoses*, VI, 388)
I

A bright clearing. Sun among the leaves,
sifting down to dapple the soft ground, and rest
a gilded bar against the muted flanks of trees.
In the glittering green light the glade
listens in and breathes.

A wooden pail; some pegs, a coil of wire;
a bundle of steel flensing knives.

Spreadeagled between two pines,
hooked at each hoof to the higher branches,
tied to the root by the hands, flagged
as his own white cross,
the satyr Marsyas hangs.

Three stand as honour guard:
two apprentices, one butcher.

II

Let's have a look at you, then.
Bit scrawny for a satyr,
all skin and whipcord, is it?
Soon find out.
So, think you can turn up with your stag-bones
and outplay Lord Apollo?
This'll learn you. Fleece the fucker.
Sternum to groin.
Tickle does it? Fucking bastard,
coming down here with your dirty ways…
Armpit to wrist, both sides.

Chasing our women…
Fine cuts round hoof and hand and neck.
Can't even speak the language proper.
Transverse from umbilicus to iliac crest,
half-circling the waist.
Jesus. You fucking stink, you do.
Hock to groin, groin to hock.
That's your inside leg done:
no more rutting for you, cunt.

Now. One of you each side.
Blade along the bone, find the tendon,
nick it and peel, nice and slow.
A bit of shirt-lifting, now, to purge him,
pull his wool over his eyes
and show him Lord Apollo's rapture;
pelt on one tree, him on another:
the inner man revealed.

III

Red Marsyas. Marsyas *écorché*,
splayed, shucked of his skin
in a tug and rift of tissue;
his birthday suit sloughed
the way a sodden overcoat is eased
off the shoulders and dumped.
All memories of a carnal life
lifted like a bad tattoo,
live bark from the vascular tree:
raw Marsyas unsheathed.

Or dragged from his own wreckage
dressed in red ropes
that plait and twine his trunk
and limbs into true definition,
he assumes the flexed pose of the hero:

the straps and buckles of ligament
glisten and tick on the sculpture
of Marsyas, muscle-man.
Mr Universe displays the map of his body:
the bulbs of high ground carved
by the curve of gully and canal,
the tributaries tight as ivy or the livid vine,
and everywhere, the purling flux of blood
in the land and the swirl of it flooding away.

Or this: the shambles of Marsyas.
The dark chest meat marbled with yellow fat,
his heart like an animal breathing
in its milky envelope,
the viscera a well-packed suitcase
of chitterlings and palpitating tripe.
A man dismantled, a tatterdemalion
torn to steak and rind,
a disappointing pentimento
or the toy that can't be reassembled
by the boy Apollo, raptor, vivisector.

The sail of stretched skin thrills and snaps
in the same breeze that makes his nerves
fire, his bare lungs scream.
Stripped of himself and from his twin:
the stiffening scab and the sticky wound.

Marsyas the martyr, a god's fetish,
hangs from the tree like bad fruit.

Carol Rumens

BEST CHINA SKY

A primrose crane, a slope of ochre stacks,
Stencilled on tissue-thin
Blue, and, flung between
These worlds, a sword-flash rainbow,
The cloud it lies against,
Metallic as its topmost skin,
And, round the eyes of hills,
The tender bluish-green
That quickly yellows.

The prism comes and goes:
Wonderful stain, transparency of art!
A smoke-wraith sails right through it.
But now it strengthens, glows and braves its span,
You'd think it was the rim
Of some resplendent turquoise plate,
Offering hills and cranes and streets and us
Fancies designed to melt
As our fingers touched them.

Lawrence Sail

ANOTHER PARTING

Remember how we gunned the car down the motorway
Towards the airport's absurdly slow
Litanies of departure? – Check-in, the catechism
Of security questions, the electric angelus
Of chimes, passport control, the gate…

When, somehow, we managed to say
Goodbye, we felt we were being crushed
By the weight of time that had massed above us
Like the grey cloud into which you would go:
And, through it all, an orphan half-phrase
Rang in my head – but a mad contradiction
Of what was real – *Time that is given*…
Today, as another parting comes closer,
The words recur, along with that cloud
Which moves over each lived minute of love.

But today those minutes have all the brightness
Of your favourite gemstones – the steady burn
Of garnets, the amethyst's clear purple,
The mallow-green of malachite, with its swirl
Of black contours beneath the surface:
As if parting itself could just be
Like seeing sunlight pinch the ocean
Into points of sparkle, or like the way
In which now that phrase finds its sudden completion –
Time that is given has no shadow.

No shadow – simply the winking grains
Of all those minutes which fire and flare
Along the runways that lead into darkness:
And, beyond, the calm patterns of the stars,
The bearings which fix our new arrivals.

Ann Sansom

Voice

Call, by all means, but just once
don't use the *broken heart again* voice;
the *I'm sick to death of life and women
and romance* voice *but with a little help
I'll try to struggle on* voice

Spare me the promise and the curse
voice, the ansafoney *Call me, please
when you get in* voice, the *nobody knows
the trouble I've seen* voice; the *I'd value
your advice* voice.

I want the how it was voice;
the *call me irresponsible but aren't I nice* voice;
the *such a bastard but I warn them in advance* voice.
The *We all have weaknesses
and mine is being wicked* voice

the *life's short and wasting time's
the only vice* voice, the s*tay in touch,
but out of reach* voice. I want to hear
the *things it's better not to broach* voice
the *things it's wiser not to voice* voice.

Carole Satyamurti

STRIKING DISTANCE

Was there one moment when the woman
who's always lived next door turned stranger
to you? In a time of fearful weather
did the way she laughed, or shook out her mats
make you suddenly feel as though
she'd been nursing a dark side to her difference
and bring that word, in a bitter rush
to the back of the throat—*Croat / Muslim /
Serb*—the name, barbed, ripping
its neat solution through common ground?

Or has she acquired an alien patina
day by uneasy day, unnoticed
as fall-out from a remote explosion?
So you don't know quite when you came to think
the way she sits, or ties her scarf,
is just like a Muslim / Serb / Croat;
and she uses their word for water-melon
as usual, but now it's an irritant
you mimic to ugliness in your head,
surprising yourself in a savage pleasure.

Do you sometimes think, she could be you,
the woman who's trying to be invisible?
Do you have to betray those old complicities
—money worries, sick children, men?
Would an open door be too much pain
if the larger bravery is beyond you
(you can't afford the kind of recklessness
that would take, any more than she could);
while your husband is saying you don't understand
those people / Serbs / Muslims / Croats?

One morning, will you ignore her greeting
and think you see a strange twist to her smile
—for how could she not, then, be strange to herself
(this woman who lives nine inches away)
in the inner place where she'd felt she belonged,
which, now, she'll return to obsessively
as a tongue tries to limit a secret sore?
And as they drive her away, will her face
be unfamiliar, her voice, bearable:
a woman crying, from a long way off?

Vernon Scannell

VIEWS AND DISTANCES

They sit together on their stolen towel
and count their few remaining francs and days
of dear vacation. Out in the bay the sea,
a crinkled spread of shimmering blue, sustains
an elegant white yacht at anchor there,
and, as they gaze, they see that, on the deck,
a man and woman have appeared who lean
languid at the vessel's rail and seem,
improbably, to offer stare for stare.

At night the sky's dark blue is deeper still,
is almost black. The rigging of the yacht
is hung with fairy-lights, and music drifts
and scents the air. The man in his white tux
and woman in her Dior gown still seem
to peer towards the shore as if they might
see once more the morning's teasing sight –
the enviable simplicities of youth
and deprivation, envy, appetite.

Jo Shapcott

VEGETABLE LOVE

I'd like to say the fridge
was clean, but look at the rusty
streaks down the back wall
and the dusty brown pools
underneath the salad crisper.

And this is where I've lived
the past two weeks, since I was pulled
from the vegetable garden.
I'm wild for him: I want to stay crunchy
enough to madden his hard palate and his tongue,
every sensitive part inside his mouth.
But almost hour by hour now, it seems,
I can feel my outer leaves losing resistance,
as oxygen leaks in, water leaks out
and the same tendency creeps further
and further towards my heart.

Down here there's not much action,
just me and another, even limper, lettuce
and half an onion. The door opens so many,
so many times a day, but he never opens
the salad drawer where I'm curled in a corner.

There's an awful lot of meat. Strange cuts:
whole limbs with their grubby hair,
wings and thighs of large birds,
claws and beaks. New juice
gathers pungency as it rolls down
through the smelly strata of the refrigerator,
and drips on to our fading heads.

The thermostat is kept as low as it will go,

and when the weather changes
for the worse, what's nearest
to the bottom of the fridge starts to freeze.
Three times we've had cold snaps,
and I've felt the terrifying pain
as ice crystals formed at my fringes.

Insulation isn't everything in here:
you've got to relax into the cold,
let it in at every pore. It's proper
for food preservation. But I heat up
again at the thought of him,
at the thought of mixing into one juice
with his saliva, of passing down his throat
and being ingested with the rest
into his body cells where I'll learn
by osmosis another lovely version
of curl, then shrivel, then open again to desire.

Penelope Shuttle

Outgrown

It is both sad and a relief to fold so carefully
her outgrown clothes and line up the little worn shoes
of childhood, so prudent, scuffed and particular.
It is both happy and horrible to send them galloping
back tappity-tap along the misty chill path into the past.

It is both a freedom and a prison, to be outgrown
by her as she towers over me as thin as a sequin
in her doc martens and her pretty skirt,
because just as I work out how to be a mother
she stops being a child.

Ken Smith

LOVESONG FOR KATE ADIE

Wherever it's bad news is where she's from –
a bronze leathery sort of lady, dressed for disaster's season,
a tough mouth woman, and like me a nighthawk. Ah, Katie,

reporting from the barbed wire rims of hell,
Katie at the barricades I dream of nightly, her voice
a bell in the desert wind, her hair blown which way.

It's true she loves it out where the disputed air
is vicious with shrapnel, bullet stung, the night's
quick stink of sulphur, flies, dead camels, terror.

But I don't mind now if she never comes back to me,
so long as she's happy. The night in her is enough,
that long-ago voice sets my gonads galloping.

Sure I'm afraid for her and pray every evening at 6
for her flight to some quiet place, cool nights
and nightingales between earthquakes and insurrections.

There we meet again, the night bright with stars:
Plough, Pleiades, Pole Star. She drinks, laughs
her special laugh, turns to go. We fall into bed.

We fuck all night, Katie & me, I never flag,
she never wearies, we're drunk on whisky and each other
and sweet fresh rocky and who cares it's Thursday?

She's there for me. I'm here for her. Any day of the week.

Sam Smith

IMPORTANT INFORMATION FOR CANOEISTS

Water exists in two planes,
the horizontal and the approximately vertical.
Umbrellas are ineffective
and interfere with the wielding of paddles.
Alligators will not be found,
although both can swim, in the same
climatic zones as elks.
Panic is started by a sudden
loss of balance. Remain seated.
Light is a commodity
and an instrument of ageing.
Jellyfish have no function
in freshwater. Neither goose nor grebe eat them.
Solitude expands the consciousness.
Loneliness makes transparent the skin.
Here you can be your identical twin.
Beaver have flat tails
and are incapable of rational conversation.
Canoes can be treacherous.
Place no reliance on shined talismans,
make sure your lifejacket is securely strapped
and trust in your own judgement.
Not to be recommended,
while afloat, under starlight or dense cloud,
is the cooking of macaroni.
Also the fermentation of blueberries
and distillation thereof, even if apricot-flavoured,
is strictly speaking illegal.
For warmth a fire of fircones
can be built at the water's edge.
(Take care not to let the parent tree
witness the incineration of its progeny.)

Coition, of whatever variety,
is best conjoined on ungiving ground.
    When following waterpaths of moorhen
and coot, be wary of contamination by crayfish.
    Be patient; and ignore
the panic-stricken flight of waterfowl.
    You are the cause.

Stephen Smith

THE EXECUTION SHED

The execution shed's 20 x 10
of unadorned scrubbed boards was built outside
B Wing; a covered annexe led the way
from the 'queer' cell which time was recessed from.
No warders were allowed to wear a watch,
a humane gesture beaten by the choice
of the word 'shed'. I looked it up; it means
outbuilding set aside from common use,
a place for beasts or implements. Language
so useful as a gloss to monitor
emotion, consecrated these bare feet.
Its primitive hygiene was like a Non-
Conformist Hut, stripped to the minimal
required for their tight ceremony.
I thought about the draughty flitching shed,
cut through by wind in Armagh, where my mother's
Da skimmed the carcasses of pigs with a wet
knife. Memories of that horror were high camp
compared to this. It is almost wicked
to research by words the final history
of this box-room. There are places that syntaxes
can't close, or conversely unlock;
where bodies devolve back before the soul;
when everything is ornamental
but the movements of the gut and a dead smell.

Jean Sprackland

DEADNETTLE

Sprawled under the hedge he snaps
the thin necks of deadnettle,
pinches the white sac, squirts
nectar into my mouth.
A small sweet promise on the tongue.

I run home in the heat. The smell
of melting tar, a stickiness underfoot.
The house whirrs and stutters with the machine.
She urges a small red dress to the needle.

She stops, examines me, stretches
to tug a snag of stickybud from my hair.
Be a good girl. She takes up the cloth

and snaps the thread on her teeth. *Won't you?*

Gillian Stoneham

ELEPHANTS

"Elephants," he shouted,
"elephants!"
from his small, bare room with the window open
on the second floor;
shouted because
elephants were what he had most wanted
all his life to see.
Neighbours and people
in the opposite street, paused
in a rattle-tattle of washing up and being busy,
to glance out of the summer-day window, paused
in their important
discussion of politics in the sitting room and
their tending of potatoes in the back garden,
and said "That
is the old man shouting again."
And his relatives
interrupted their thoughts for just a moment
to sigh with resignation.
But no-one attempted to go and look
in the small square room
where the old man sat on the edge of his bed
smiling and satisfied,
as the elephants, ponderous but gentle
walked round and round, snuffing the air
with their curious trunks, and treading
ever so softly.

Matthew Sweeney

INCIDENT IN EXETER STATION
for Eddie Linden

He came in the door, staring at me,
like he'd known me in another life.
'I've chased everywhere after you,' he said.
'Years and years, I've been on the road,
too many to count. The train-fares,
the bus-fares, the plane-fares. . .
The least you can do is buy me a pint.'
He plonked his duffle-bag on the floor
and sat on the stool next to mine.
He looked in my eyes like a holy man,
said 'You're looking well, you've lost weight.'
His face could have done with flesh.
His hair needed a cut and a wash.
'I don't know you,' I said, 'I've never,
ever seen you before.' He smiled,
the same smile Jesus must have flashed
at Judas, then his face changed
into a voodoo mask, as he shouted
'After all I've done for you!',
turning to face the roomful of eaters
and drinkers, all of whom ignored him
but I knew they classed us together,
so, seeing a train pull up at the platform,
I grabbed my hat, bags and ran,
getting in just as the train was leaving,
not knowing where it was headed,
hearing his roars follow me out
into the green Devon countryside
that I'd never risk visiting again.

George Szirtes

BACKWATERS: NORFOLK FIELDS
for W G Sebald

1
Backwaters. Long grass. Slow speech. Far off
a truck heaves its load of rust into a yard
next to a warehouse full of office furniture
no one will ever use, unless to stuff
some temporary room when times are hard.
Across the fields the sweet smell of manure.

We're years behind. Even our vowels sag
in the cold wind. We have our beauty spots
that people visit and leave alone, down main
arterials and side roads. A paper bag
floats along the beach. Clouds drift in clots
of grey and eventually down comes the rain.

We're at the end. It might simply be of weather
or empire or of something else altogether.

2
Empire perhaps. Chapels in the cathedral.
Old airstrips. History's human noises
still revving down a field. Clothes pegs hang
like hanged men. It is all procedural.
Resentment simmers in the empty houses.
The wind at its eternal droning harangue.

I'm wanting to mouth the word that fits the case
but it's like trying to roll a shadow from
the street where it has been sitting for years.
It will not go. You cannot wipe the face
of the clock or restore a vanished kingdom.

You feel the shape of the thing between your ears.

Your mouth is talking to the steady light
which listens to you and remains polite.

3
How beautiful the place is. Watch it hold
time still. I want you to tell me what this is,
this place at the back of beyond, in the sun
that retains its distance in a pale gold
mirror, minding its own brilliant business,
not in the habit of speaking to anyone.

Here is a man who loves cars. He has bought
a house on something very like a hill.
He fills his yard up with old cars. He mends things –
roofs, walls. He's biblical. He does not take thought
for the morrow, won't worry when he falls ill.
He goes swooping along on welded wings,

his children unruly, his wife losing heart.
The beautiful is what keeps them apart.

4
The WI stall. Jams, flowers. White
hair scraped back in the draught of an open door.
The butcher's. He knows you by name. He calls
your name out. His chopping block is washed bright
by the morning sun. The solicitor
down the street. His nameplate. War memorials

with more names. Rows of Standleys, Bunns,
Myhills, Kerridges. Names on shopfronts: bold
reds, whites and blues in stock typography.
Names on labels tied with string to shotguns.

Names on electoral registers. Names in gold
in the children's section of the cemetery

by the railway cutting. Willows, faint blue
in the afternoon, light gently whistles through.

5
Too easy all this, like a fatal charm
intended to lull you into acquiescence.
Think karaoke. Sky. The video shop.
Broken windows. The sheer boredom. The alarm
wailing at two a.m. The police presence.
Pastoral graffiti on the bus stop.

Think back of the back of beyond 'beyond'. End
of a line. The sheer ravishing beauty
of it as it runs into the cold swell
of the North Sea, impossible to comprehend.
The harsh home truisms of geometry
that flatten to a simple parallel.

This is your otherness where the exotic
appears by a kind of homely conjuring trick.

6
A fifteen-eighties mural. A hunting scene
runs right around the room. A trace of Rubens,
Jordaens, a touch, even, of Chinese
in the calligraphic lines. Experts clean
the powdery limewash, two PhD students
from the university, anxious to please.

A strange dome appears, out of period
somewhere near the top. Even here
there's something far flung in the code

of a different language, another God
extolling other virtues, a pioneer
morality just waiting to explode.

Flemish brickwork. Devastation. Riders
exploring hidden walls with snails and spiders.

7

You're out at the end of the pier. It is winter.
Tall waves splutter underfoot. Gulls pirouette
and dive into dark grey. The radio is alive
with music. Its tiny voices seem to splinter
into sharp distinct consonants. You forget
the time of day. It's someone else's narrative

buzzing beneath you. New explorers come
out of the light to exploit the heart of darkness.
The world is inside out, exposed as never before.
Water and sky are a continuum.
A terrible gaiety rustles the sea like a dress
it must discard. It sweeps by just once more

then drops across the beach and remains there
in the memory, in ghosted, mangled air.

8

How beautiful it is, this silence waiting
on salt. The disused railway lines between
wild blackberries. The faint hum of stray flies
on windowsills. Time is accelerating
down the coast road leaving behind a clean
pair of heels and a whiff of paradise.

The man with welded wings roars past, in love
with reason. His wife leaves in a freak gust,

their children flying along. Dogs race across
the walls in search of a lost treasure trove.
Gently idling, vast trucks deposit rust
in empty yards with patches of dry grass.

Broad fields out of town. The slow unravelling
of a long reel where everyone is travelling.

9
Travelling through or ending. The damp house
beyond the library where an old woman
has been retreating for some fifty years,
and still retreats towards a dangerous
blind alley, towards a corner, where the nearest demon
might swallow her up leaving no more tears.

There are none left to shed in the overgrown
garden with its coarse weeds. It is as if
she had been sleeping a century or more,
without a retinue, simply on her own,
growing ever more querulous, ever more stiff
till rigor mortis had frozen her four score

into zero. Country aristocracy.
The dead fields at their last-gasp fantasy.

10
A place full of old women. Hardy, courageous,
muttering to themselves and others in cafés,
engaging unwilling partners in conversation,
accosting young men, making outrageous
advances to middle-aged couples with tea-trays,
embarrassing husbands with their ostentation.

Old men in betting shops peering to check

the odds. Old men, natty in white, creaking
over bowls, with Beryl Cook elegance.
Old men tottering, sticking out a neck
at the neighbour while the latter is speaking.
Old men in the church hall learning to dance.

The old in their gerontopolis. At home
in sheltered housing, under the pleasure dome.

11
How many times do I have to say the word: End!
and still not end. You can't go further than
the sea, not on a motorway. And what
are you doing here, yes, you and your friend
from Morocco, Uganda, St. Kitts or Pakistan?
Whatever has brought you to this far, flat

kingdom with its glum farmers! Surely you
don't think this is America where dreams
are the given, where you swear allegiance
to a new self? Have you somehow fallen through
the net of the world to be lost among reams
of legislature in these alien regions?

Homing. We are homing to the sea. Back
where we never were, at the end of the track.

12
On a high-cloud day, you could drown in sky
round here. You see the gentle swaying
of leaves along a wall. Something under
the water, under the sky-light, in the dry
cabin under the ocean is quietly playing
a music of muted bells in soft thunder.

It is eating you away until you've gone,
like the spider scurrying up its own spit
back to its natural centre in the dark.
And the sky remains enormous. Someone
is watching the house-martin, the blue tit,
the tiny insects making their tiny mark

in the grass, and the small rain that falls far
across the field as on a distant star.

R S Thomas

What god is proud
    of this garden
of dead flowers, this underwater
    grotto of humanity,
where limbs wave in invisible
    currents, faces drooping
on dry stalks, voices clawing
    in a last desperate effort
to retain hold? Despite withered
    petals, I recognise
the species: Charcot, Ménière,
    Alzheimer. There are no gardeners
here, caretakers only
    of reason overgrown
by confusion. This body once,
    when it was in bud,
opened to love's kisses. These eyes,
    cloudy with rheum,
were clear pebbles that love's rivulet
    hurried over. Is this
the best Rabbi Ben Ezra
    promised? I come away
comforting myself, as I can,
    that there is another
garden, all dew and fragrance,
    and that these are the brambles
about it we are caught in,
    a sacrifice prepared
by a torn god to a love fiercer
    than we can understand.

Charles Thomson

We saved our Persil coupons
   and from Maidstone caught a train
to spend the day beside the sea
   at Ramsgate, in the rain.

We took our lunch in a café
   and we took up smoking again
and we took a stroll for souvenirs
   from Ramsgate, in the rain.

We went into the amusement arcade
   where the videos addle the brain,
and we looked at the little harbour
   of Ramsgate, in the rain.

It was really rather romantic,
   though the sky was a great grey stain,
to spend last Sunday with you
   in Ramsgate, in the rain.

John Powell Ward

SPELLING

Is he still it now? Is Jesus
It now, or has it changed now? Is

Jesus still it now, King of
Jews like and the world now? Is he

King now still like they said, like we
Kids were told, is he king still of

Love now, like when in the bombs and
Later the rationing, is he son of

Man as they said or at least
Many said, or some said? Oh. He's

Not now. That's all over and done
Now, that's it then. Oh, right,

Oh, so it's over now. Oh well, it's
Over and gone now. Too bad then. Oh.

Andrew Waterhouse

Looking for the Comet

You push back the sheet, leave me
naked and cooling in the night air.
You stand by the window,
by the yellow flowers in their blue vase
and there's moon on your face and shoulders.
"It's here," you say, but I'm pretending sleep,
and just watch you, watching the comet
moving off towards the sun and beyond.

A car passes. Headlights fill the window,
making new shadows, that rise, then fall.
You take a flower from the vase,
carry it to me in both hands, slowly wipe
the petals over my face. Now, I can smell
the pollen on my skin, feel the trail.

Susan Wicks

MY FATHER IS SHRINKING

When we last hugged each other
in the garage,
our two heads were level.
Over his shoulder I could see
potato-sacks.

Another season
and in the dusty sunlight
I shall gather him to me,
smooth his collar,
bend to listen
for his precious breathing.

When he reaches
to my waist,
I shall no longer
detach his small hands
from my skirt,
escape his shrill voice
in the dawn garden.

When he comes to my knees,
I shall pick him up and rock him,
rub my face on the white
stubble of his cheek,
see his silver skull
gleam up at me
through thin combings.

C K Williams

1

All under the supposition that he's helping her because she's so
    often melancholy lately,
he's pointing out certain problems with her character, but he's so
    serious, so vehement,
she realizes he's *attacking* her, to hurt, not help; she doesn't know
    what might be driving him,
but she finds she's thinking through his life for him, the losses,
    the long-forgotten sadnesses,
and though she can't come up with anything to correlate with
    how hatefully he's acting,
she thinks *something* has to be there, so she listens, nods, some-
    times she actually agrees.

2

They're only arguing, but all at once she feels anxiety, and real-
    izes she's afraid of him,
then, wondering whether she should risk expressing it to him,
    she understands she can't,
that the way he is these days he'll turn it back on her, and so she
    keeps it to herself,
then, despite herself, she wonders what their life's become to
    have to hide so much,
then comes a wave of disappointment, with herself, not him, and
    not for that initial fear,
but for some cowardice, some deeper dread that makes her ask,
    why not him?

3

He's very distant, but when she asks him what it is, he insists it's
    nothing, though it's not,
she knows it's not, because he never seems to face her and his
    eyes won't hold on hers;
it makes her feel uncertain, clumsy, then as though she's some-
    how supplicating him:
though she wants nothing more from him than she already has –
    what would he think she'd want? –
when she tries to trust him, to believe his offhanded reassurance,
    she feels that she's pretending,
it's like a game, though very serious, like trying to talk yourself
    out of an imminent illness.

4

If there are sides to take, he'll take the other side, against any-
    thing she says, to anyone:
at first she thinks it's just coincidence; after all, she knows she's
    sometimes wrong,
everyone is sometimes wrong, but with him now all there seem
    to be are sides, she's always wrong;
even when she doesn't know she's arguing, when she doesn't
    care, he finds her wrong,
in herself it seems she's wrong, she feels she should apologize, to
    someone, anyone, to him;
him, him, him; what is it that he wants from her: remorse, con-
    trition, should she just *die*?

5

He's telling her in much too intricate detail about a film he's
    seen: she tries to change the subject,
he won't let her, and she finds she's questioning herself – must
    she be so critical, judgmental? –

then she's struck, from something in his tone, or absent from his
        tone, some lack of resonance,
that why he's going on about the movie is because there's noth-
        ing else to say to her,
or, worse, that there are things to say but not to her, they're too
        intimate to waste on her:
it's *she*, she thinks, who's being measured and found wanting, and
        what should she think now?

      6

This time her, her story, about something nearly noble she once
        did, a friend in trouble,
and she helped, but before she's hardly started he's made clear he
        thinks it's all a fantasy,
and she as quickly understands that what he really means is that
        her love, her love for him,
should reflexively surpass the way she loved, or claims she loved,
        the long-forgotten friend,
and with a shock of sorrow, she knows she can't tell him that,
        that the betrayal,
and certainly there is one, isn't his desire to wound, but her
        thinking that he shouldn't.

      7

She sits in his lap, she's feeling lonely, nothing serious, she just
        wants sympathy, company,
then she realizes that though she hasn't said a word, he's sensed
        her sadness and is irked,
feels that she's inflicting, as she always does, he seems to think,
        her misery on him,

so she tells herself not to be so needy anymore, for now, though, she just wants to leave,

except she can't, she knows that if he suspects he's let her down he'll be more irritated still,

and so she stays, feeling dumb and out of place, and heavy, heavier, like a load of stone.

8

She experiences a pleasurable wave of nostalgia, not for her own past, but for his:

she can sense and taste the volume and the textures of the room he slept in as a child,

until she reminds herself she's never been there, never even seen the place, so, reluctantly,

she thinks reluctantly, she wonders if she might not be too close, too devoted to him,

whether she might actually be trying to become him, then she feels herself resolve, to her surprise,

to disengage from him, and such a sense of tiredness takes her that she almost cries.

9

As usual these days he's angry with her, and because she wants him not to be she kisses him,

but perhaps because he's so surprised, she feels him feel her kiss came from some counter-anger,

then she starts to doubt herself, wondering if she might have meant it as he thinks she did,

as a traitor kiss, a Judas kiss, and if that's true, his anger, both his angers, would be justified:

look, though, how he looks at her, with bemusement, hardly hidden, he knows her so well,

he senses her perplexity, her swell of guilt and doubt: how he cherishes his wrath!

10

Such matters end, there are healings, breakings-free; she tells
      herself they end, but still,
years later, when the call she'd dreaded comes, when he calls,
      asking why she hasn't called,
as though all those years it wasn't her who'd called, then stopped
      calling and began to wait,
then stopped waiting, healed, broke free, so when he innocently
      suggests they get together,
she says absolutely not, but feels uncertain – is she being spiteful?
      small? – and then she knows:
after this he'll cause her no more pain, though no matter how
      she wished it weren't, this is pain.

Frances Williams

OYSTER EATING

Luxury doesn't get more
Astringent. Plucked from
Cloudy depths, my plate
Of oysters wait for their
Moment, little glaciers
In silky cups. I suck

An avalanche of flesh.
Then clear my throat
Of their strange salt
Swallow, more touch
Than taste. Out of these
Rocky skulls, the brains

Come slippery as sex.
Each one tips over the
Rugged callused lips of
Its single shoe to speak
Only with the one tongue,
A probe both first and

Last. Such rash
Adventurers. Jonahs
In my whale. And also
Something sad in our
Hurried consummation.
A dozen down, I reach

A check-mate moment
In this game of numbers.
As Casanova, on a lucky
Night, might break a line
Of kisses, to pause for breath
On heaven's racing staircase.

Hugo Williams

Joy

Not so much a sting
as a faint burn

not so much a pain
as the memory of pain

the memory of tears
flowing freely down cheeks

in a sort of joy
that there was nothing

worse in all the world
than stinging nettle stings

and nothing better
than cool dock leaves.

Edna Wyley

Books, Poetry in the Making

My father always kept his books clean.
When reading, he balanced those precious words
on his table of well-ironed corduroy thighs
and advised that like him I be careful to touch
with two fingers (quite briefly)
only the corners of each finished page
when ready to move on –
though often I would watch his hand
slowly feel across the turning thoughts,
like a man's light touch in reluctant farewell
of a face he has come to love.

Mine were the new but battered ones,
covers bent far back, edges creased.
"It's beyond me how you can manage
to mangle everyone", he'd taunt –
but I was finding in each mauled book
a home for my own ways; I liked sand
shifting where the pages joined in story,
breadcrumbs long left over
suddenly flaking free from words,
and split hairs forked above lines
as a diviner's stock over water –
all meant more than any signature to me,
that these books were mine.

Mine, marked with breakfast coffee spilt
on the earliest 50A ride to work,
the back seat windows
my jolting, smogged up pillows
while words unstuck the sleep in my eyes.

He sat with his books in our sitting room –

one finger pressed each line to life
while his tongue between teeth
wet his upper lip.

Closed, he marked them
with old card greetings
or writings from St. John
he'd discovered that February
early in his fortieth year.
He never drank or smoked again
but he still takes Marx down
from his full book shelf
arranged in Library order.
He was ever suspicious and knew
which ones had gone missing,
borrowed when I hoped he wasn't looking.

Just when he had no need to worry,
he chose my leave of home
to hide the books
behind his wardrobe door – the titles
like his absent daughter's name
he could never say again
without remembering too much.
Father, we will meet, surprised, someday,
both reaching for the same line.

Benjamin Zephaniah

MAN TO MAN

Macho man
Can't cook
Macho man
Can't sew
Macho man
Eats plenty Red Meat,
At home him is King,
From front garden to back garden
From de lift to de balcony
Him a supreme Master,
Controller.

Food mus ready
On time,
Cloth mus ready
On time,
Woman mus ready
On time,
How Macho can yu go?

Cum
Talk to me bout sexuality,
Cum meditate,
Cum Save de Whale,
Dose bulging muscles need Tai Chi
Yu drunken eyes need herb tea,
Cum, Relax.

Macho man
Can't cook, sew or wash him pants,
But Macho Man is in full control.